THE FILMS OF
SOPHIA LOREN

THE FILMS OF
SOPHIA LOREN

By Tony Crawley

Citadel Press   Secaucus, N.J.

Acknowledgements

While grateful acknowledgement is duly accorded to all film companies concerned, and full credits given to my Press colleagues quoted within (British and American only; we *know* the E.E.C. adores Sophia, so it seems more apposite to note her impact on Anglo-Saxons), I also have to thank various friends and acquaintances, in and out of Wardour Street, for their kind and speedy assistance during my first leap into the deep-end. Such life-belts are really too numerous to name, but must include: the tireless B.F.I. librarians; Tom Carlile; Barbara De Lord; Carol Futrall; Colin Hankins; Mary Herscott; Alan Hutchinson; Patsy Kelly; Joy Maitland; Leslie Pound; Hugh Samson; Frank Selby; Julian Senior; Graham Smith; Alan Wheatley; and Nicole, Nicholas, Delphine, for alarm-clocks, sustenance, support. Extra thanks also to Jean-Claude Missiaen in Paris; Walter Alford in Rome; John Kobal, obviously, in London (without whose fervour so many historic stills would grace trash-cans only); and, of course, the gracious Ms. Loren herself.

First American Edition, 1976
Copyright© 1974 by LSP Books Limited
All rights reserved
Published by Citadel Press
A division of Lyle Stuart, Inc.
120 Enterprise Ave., Secaucus, N. J. 07094
Manufactured in the United States of America

Edited by Tom Hutchinson
Designed by Jeff Tarry

ISBN-0-8065-0512-5

Dedicated with thanks
for the memory of

Adelina, Adriana, Agnese, Aida, Aldonza, Angela,
Anna, Antoinette, Barbara, Carmela, Caterine,
Catherine, Cesira, Chimene, Cinzia, Cleopatra,
Dita, Dulcinea, Epifania, Filumena, Germana,
Giovanna, Honoria, Isabella, Johanna, Juana,
Judith, Kay, Lina, Lisa, Lucia, Lucilla, Louise,
Maddalena, Mara, Maria, Natascha, Nisca, Nives,
Nora, Olympia, Phaedra, Rose, Sisina, Sofia, Stella,
Teresa, Valerie, Yasmin, Zoe

—to the soul of them all,
Sophia Loren

Contents

Sketch of Sophia by Hollywood director Jean Negulesco; circa 1957.

Sophia Loren, Body & Soul —la diva popolana

'What is Sophia, who is she? She is sunlight, she is hearty warmth, she is great contentment with simple things. She is song and laughter, dance. She is a free-hearted lover, yet never depraved. The wonder is that although she could not possibly exist, there she is: existing. She is not fake.'—Stanley Kaufman, The New Republic.

Sophia Loren is Horatio Alger, Italian style. In an industry created to manufacture dreams and spew out old players for new with relentless regurgitation, she has survived 25 years, from lowly 'extra' to luminous legend, living out the biggest drama of all: *scunizzi*, or street-urchin, into the world's most durable and desired movie queen and actress.

Born into Mussolini's fascist Italy, she has grown in beauty, stature, style—above all, that commanding Style—personality and years to see her sister marry the ex-Duce's son; brought up a ferry ride from the glistening Capri, too poor ever to afford the trip, she returned to be guided around the enchanting isle by no less a cinematic god than Clark Gable; raised in a hell and hail of bombs, blood, tears and *miseria*, she has drawn upon and from that most bitter childhood to win the first Hollywood Oscar ever awarded to a foreign actress in a foreign-language film; and battling both her nation and her church, she finally married the one man she loved and then, due to the formidable riches both attained in their fantasy-filled world of cinema, she was able to give birth to the children that it had seemed for so long she was physically incapable of carrying and bearing.

Cinderella, Italian style, then. Which, aptly enough, became the British title for one of her films *napoletana*. The project, a fairy story starring a genuine fairy story, lost its magic charm at the box-office; but there is no more suitable sub-title for the life of Loren.

From sharing a bed with two grandparents and a maiden aunt to owning several plush homes scattered around Europe, including a veritable palace in her sumptuous 50-roomed, 16th-century villa at Marino, near Rome, is pure Cinders copy. With her voluptuous shape—a face and frame she admits to be 'a unity of irregularities'; legs that talk; Etruscan eyes that sigh; and all-over Vesuvian contours, only out-deafened in their clarion call to arms by the over-generous appeal to the senses when the complete equipment is viewed in a vision of motion— she is, most definitely, definitively, Italian: Neapolitan! As for style ... ah! If only they could bottle it! She is truly gifted in all facets of the kind of stellar Style already trickling out of screen fashion when she was an extra, and which she, alone among the post-war superlegends, continues to impart—in her own incandescent, shimmering way.

Her feet, though, have rarely strayed far from the ground. She may well be the stuff that superlative dreams are made of; she may be at once both fantasy and reality. Yet she knows her roots. From first to last in a career of sparkling enjoyment, rich in Neapolitan laughter and tears, Sophia Loren has remained *la diva popolana*. A star of the people: for the people and by the people.

Her life is probably better known than that of any other living post-war discovery. Her followers must know her childhood better than their own. Few have not heard at least something of her illegitimate birth, miserable youth in war-time Pozzuoli, even the cruel cat-calls of her schooldays: *figlia naturale* (lovechild) and *stuzzicadente* (tooth-pick). Her story has been more fully documented than many a real queen, re-written, rejigged, revaluated, causing almost as many factoids as the Monroe life, and aired almost as constantly as that of Michael Caine. To, perhaps, far better purpose.

For Sophia remains one of the precious few superstars who never forgets where she came from; indeed it could be said, she never lets her audience forget it either. 'I always tell the truth. I cannot be bothered to lie—you need such a good memory. So

I tell the truth about what I think, about my past, about my father. Peace of mind is what is most important to me. If I tell lies I would destroy it. So it is the truth or nothing. I can't help it if I shock people. They must like me for what I am—not what I pretend to be.' Which is why she is so popular in Europe, and why she is at her finest when filming on local territory. 'I hope—in vain, I know—that Miss Loren will never make films outside Italy,' the American critic Stanley Kaufman wrote of her *Two Women* triumph. 'On her own ground ... and especially with the help of De Sica, she is splendid.'

Loren agrees. 'Nobody can forget that I am Italian and, of course, when I work in Italy I feel much more at home than when abroad. But in some films I did very nice things out of Italy. For instance, *The Key* —that I adore very much. And even that wonderful story that unfortunately was made too much on the set—it should have been made differently, more on location—that beautiful story of O'Neill, *Desire Under The Elms*. *Black Orchid*, too, was a good film. And *Man of La Mancha* was a wonderful experience for me. But I have to admit my own favourites are particularly *Two Women*—oh! I never thought it would be as great as that! And I loved *Marriage, Italian Style* and *Yesterday, Today and Tomorrow*—fun to make!'

Unquenchable as a Neapolitan ('in Naples, anything can happen!'), she has adroitly reconnoitred all parts, all genres, and quite a few nationalities, though three only of her characters have been minus the inevitable final vowel-*italiano*. In the hands of various directors, both careful and careless, she displays the pre-eminent gifts of a born survivor, successive proficiency in any dramatic compartment that intrigues her, and total acceptability as princess or prostitute, sophisticate or wild-cat.

In common with all cinema's grand stars (it could be termed the only *common* trait about her), her 67-film career has been a constant fusion of reality and reel-ity. Scripts forever mirror aspects of her personal experience: the *scunizzi* cowering from war-bombing in a cupboard in *Marriage, Italian Style*; the accidental model having the Eliza Dolittle treatment to the big time in *Lucky To Be a Woman*; the well-built beauty beset by unwanted male admirers in *The Sign of Venus*; the wife discovering she has a bigamous husband in *Sunflower*; the succession of mothers she craved so desperately to be herself; and, of course, the hand-hewn memoirs of something as strongly traumatic as *Two Women*. Or in the more basic and usually comedic Loren vehicle, reporting the rise of a working-class heroine, pizza-seller/eel-cutter/sponge-diver/seamstress/laundress/call-girl/factory-hand/rock-singer to something loftier, whether countess, princess, duchess or simply adored wife

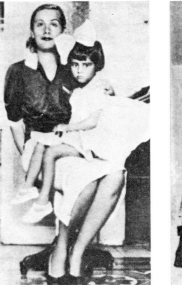

Childhood. Sofia Scicolone, thin and serious aged three, sits on Mamina's lap in the little red house at Pozzuoli. There she played with cardboard stage-costume cut-outs and studied piano under her mother's instructive eye. At 12 (top right), she was still called a 'little stick'; within a couple of years she began to bloom, flower and positively glow.

and beloved mother.

Nothing, though, ever untoward, censorial; the sole *breath of scandal* in her story was a film of that name ... and a few other flops like it clouding her aura.

Soon after she gained some initial prominence, there started the much-headlined, astutely staged rivalry with the then leading bosom of Italian movies, Gina Lollobrigida; next came a French foe in the continually undraped shape of Brigitte Bardot; and the Rome feud, much more one-sided, from Italy's screen *mamma*, Anna Magnani. Loren out-paced, out-classed, out-lasted them all, in rapid succession and with astonishing precision. By 1954, more than 100,000 girls—reported by *Newsweek* to be three per cent of the female Italian population between 16 and 26—were entering beauty contests in attempts to follow Loren to the top. Of rivals she had plenty. Home-grown aspirants like Marisa Allasio, Sandra Milo, Claudia Cardinale, Daniela Rocca, Elsa Martinelli. Importees galore: Daliah Lavi, Sylva Koscina, Belinda Lee, Margaret Lee, Abbe Lane, Mara and Jackie Lane, Anne Heywood, and even ex-Hollywoodians Joan Collins and Carroll Baker. They, too, were swiftly left far behind. Basically, they all overacted. Loren merely re-acted—to herself, to her own true persona and to the winning dichotomy of symbol and reality.

She is a star more than an actress, and more devastating still as an intoxicating comedienne: the finest in Europe, if not the world. Pauline Kael has called her a gorgeous funny woman: 'wouldn't we rather watch her than better actresses because she's so incredibly charming and because she's probably the greatest model the world has ever known.' Vittorio De Sica—and who knows her better among directors?—says she is a *filodrammatica*, an amateur actress with beauty and talent—'but she needs to be handled'. He does it best and has helped make her a monument, embodying all Italy's strengths in much the same fashion as someone as fragile as Monroe conjured up America's weaknesses.

Sophia, for example, has never seriously been taken for a vamp. Once the initial onslaught of her sex-symbolical pin-ups died down, women appreciated her talents every bit as men. Women see no rival in the Loren imagery, they lose no menfolk to her shrine—she is no teaser; every promise is delivered. Sophia is for real. She exists. She *is*. And what they do see, these women, is themselves; what, with that little extra slice of good fortune, they could be, that which they want to be. There are those critics, myself among them, who later complained when her image ascended from earth mother to queen mother (complete with those manicured eyebrows). The sheer, dishy, dazzling essence that is Loren stayed true and constant, all the same. Woman! *La donna popolana*.

Early publicity used to have her saying: 'I was born in the Clinica Margherita ...' Sophia sticks to the truth. The screen's best-loved Neapolitan was born, far from the city slicker limits, in the city hospital, the Rome Policlinicio, on September 20, 1934,* and the doctors soon advised her 20-year-old mother, Romilda Villani, to take the infant Sophia (or Sofia Villani Scicolone as she was named), to warmer climes. They trekked south to Pozzuoli, a squalid industrial suburb and port north of Naples, and

Pride. Sofia, still thin, on her First Communion day.

moved in with her maternal grandparents in the second-floor flat at 5 Via Solfatara. It was a typical Napoli household: overcrowded. Seven people, soon to be nine, stuffed into two bedrooms, kitchen and dining-room. An aunt shared one bedroom with her labourer husband; the rest squeezed into the other, Sophia sleeping with her Mamina in a small bed, until her sister arrived when she had to join both grandparents and another aunt in the other, fortunately 'big, big' bed in the room. Grandfather Domenico Villani was a foreman at the Ansaldo munitions factory and the thin little girl's days were, more often than not, spent with granny in the

* For the record, 8 days later her eventual rival, Brigitte Bardot, was born in Paris.

11

kitchen. Bread and bean soup (*minestrina*) every morning; pasta with something at night; and, if lucky, meat in 'the sacred stew' every Sunday after Mass at the Madonna del Carmine church.

'I was born old,' Loren has said. 'I never had a childhood.' Mamina agrees: both daughters were like little women when they were born. Apart from the crowded bed and her mother giving piano lessons, Sophia recalls little else. Romilda, a striking, tall redhead, passed on both looks and aspirations to her daughter; Mamina had studied at the music conservatoire at Naples, once played *Queen Christina* on the stage, and even won a Garbo look-alike contest to go to Hollywood and work as the star's double. Her mother refused her permission because of what happened to Valentino in America. 'They poisoned him,' said Loren's grandmother. (In 1973, Sophia was the third recipient of the Rudolph Valentino Prize as 'an artist whose personality has conquered the world in the same way as Valentino'. The ceremony took place in the Latin Lover's birthplace, the ancient city of Lecce, in Italy's south-east province of Puglia; honoured at the same event was her three times co-star, Anthony Quinn. The trophy had only been initiated the year before when the first winners were Elizabeth Taylor and Richard Burton.)

Loren's father, a construction engineer named Riccardo Scicolone, was rarely in evidence at the little red house and then only in answer to her mother's fake cables: 'Sofia seriously ill. Come at once.' When he did turn up, Sophia recalls, he was 'like a donkey at a concert' and she would petulantly refuse to acknowledge him, calling her grandfather Papa, in preference. Scicolone was married with two sons in Rome; tall, strong, distinguished-looking, his daughter once described him, with a beautiful smile, rather haughty, with great charm. Enough to provide Sophia with a sister, Maria, in 1937.

'He was present just enough to give me complexes,' Loren told novelist Alberto Moravia in an interview discussing her illegitimacy. 'It made me ashamed ... that I did not have a normal family. Especially at school where the other girls could talk about their fathers and I couldn't. He simply took no account of me. It made me work very young so that I could not just tell him but show him I didn't want to be a schoolteacher.'

By five, she had started in the local elementary school, a trifle undisciplined, a bit of a dreamer. At home she would play with Maria, making up stories on the kitchen table with cardboard cut-outs of stage costumes. If life had not been idyllic, it was to get

Sofia Lazzaro, The Vamp of the *fumetti* romance and adventure picture magazines. Vastly popular in Italy, these foto-strips never caught on in Britain or the States, where a comic is a comic is a comic. *Tit-Bits* magazine, however, did try a few strips—with Loren plainly recognisable ... even as a heroine named Meg McKenna!

These foto-strips are reproduced by kind permission of *Tit-Bits*.

very much worse. The war arrived on their doorstep. Food virtually disappeared. 'It wasn't just poverty, it was *miseria*.' Spaghetti proved the staple diet (and how she must have sent sales soaring within a few years when she claimed all she had, she owed to spaghetti). All food was scarce, black-marketed, and had to be queued for in a bread-line. Air raids occurred three or four times a night—in the day too, which meant 'missing places in the food-line if you went for shelter'—and the family spent nights cooped up with neighbours in the dark, safe but suffocatingly smelly air of the Pozzuoli railway tunnel; and then until 4 a.m. only, as the first train came through at 4.15.

Poverty may spur ambition, the star was to agree in happier days, but it also made people angry. 'I grew up to the sound of anger and screams. I try and try but I can never remember the happy times that must have happened in my childhood. Exploding bombs left me stretched out on the floor in a cold sweat. I used to lie there wondering what would become of me ... Nowadays it all seems as if it happened to another person.'

Pozzuoli then became in direct line of fire from the Allied ships, and amid the total chaos of one army's advance and another's retreat, the entire population was evacuated to Naples in the summer of '43, there to join the hundreds living on Monte Sarno. Romilda's account of the ten-kilometre trail to Napoli reads like this, exactly like *Two Women*: 'The only time I actually begged for food was when we were in Naples. Both my girls had fever. The Germans were pulling out and I was watching the flashes in the sky when I saw a woman in another house holding a piece of bread in her hands. I begged that piece of bread from her ... I felt awful at that moment. My face went red with shame, but my babies were starving and I just had to do it.' Sophia, too, has vague memories of the day when her mother, all resistance gone, cried out for bread—and syphoned water from a car's radiator.

Slowly, the horror that is war passed them by and Pozzuoli was occupied once more—by its people. Naples was liberated in 1944 and Sophia saw her first Allied soldier, a kilted Scot. 'I laughed so hard at a man in a skirt, I got a pain in my stomach.' It was a sight to bring laughter back to many a *scunizzi* urchin of the *generazione bruciata*: the burnt generation. Back the family went to the little red house, its windows blown out and every room in shambles. Life was not hard any more, it was intolerable. No food still, no work either. And by now there were nine in the four rooms. The married aunt and uncle had their own child; Maria had typhoid; Sophia showed all the signs of the ravaged years. *Lo stecchino*, they called her at school: little stick. The Allies came to the rescue with food parcels. 'I think,' says Sophia, 'we would have starved to death if it hadn't been for the American G.I.s.'

She had, though, already shown her vast instinct for

survival, coming through the war with (physically) nothing more than a scar on her chin, after crashing down on some rocks during one headlong dash for the safety of the rail-tunnel in a raid. The war halted, and whether from the slowly increasing food or the callisthenics at school, the little stick became a tree: tall and willowy, wonderfully so. The girl became a woman between 13 and 14; it became a pleasure to stroll down the street, and the crowds watching the gym work-outs at the open-air ancient amphitheatre grew noticeably larger. At 14 she had her first marriage proposal from, appropriately enough, the gym instructor. 'Mamina shooed him out of the house in two seconds!'

Rather than boys, the young Sophia had, like the rest of her generation, discovered the magic of cinema. 'I adored the films I started to see in Pozzuoli after 1945, when we started to get American films once again. That was the big boom of Rita Hayworth, Betty Grable, even Ginger Rogers and Fred Astaire. Of Linda Darnell, Tyrone Power … and Cary Grant! That was the kind of picture I liked. I loved very much going to the movies and if I liked the film I would stay for two or three shows until they closed the cinema. My aunt didn't like that very much. That meant I was home late—and I was still very little.'

Tit-Bits foto-strip, continued from previous page.

Sophia was still 14 when she began creating her own legend. A beauty contest was announced in Naples, to find a Queen of the Seas. In all, some 365 participants were expected, Sofia Scicolone among them, causing a definite *bisticcio familiare* row at home. Romilda alone approved the idea, until the prize money was discussed, when everyone buckled down to help Sophia. An evening gown and shoes were required—who wore shoes any more? Grandmother supplied some rose material, and the shoes came from Mamina. Sophia, not yet a queen, was voted as one of a dozen princesses winning 25,000 lire, a bolt of cloth, a table service and some wallpaper—which stayed upon grandfather Domenico's walls for the next couple of decades.

The school friends jibed some more, and to give her daughter confidence more than a career, Romilda entered her in a tiny local dramatic school. Meanwhile, the news from Rome was of the new promised land of Cinecitta. Hollywood on the Tiber was happening, *Quo Vadis* was about to start, thousands of extras were required and all those dollars just waiting to be grabbed. Mamina gambled everything on a hunch, spent the last of the beauty contest money on two third-class tickets to Rome, to seek their fortunes. Which for women in 1950 in Italy meant the movies.

De Sica should have been around to record their entry into Rome. They created their own neo-realistic

tragi-comedy. Arriving with barely a sou, wearing or carrying all they owned, Romilda actually phoned director Mervyn LeRoy—and got through to him!—and he agreed to see them as he was looking for a young girl who could speak English. They found refuge with some relatives but had no luck in obtaining financial support from Scicolone. (He actually called in the police because Sophia was a minor, and he wanted both back out of harm's way in the South.) They turned up next day at Cinecitta auditions and when announcing her name as Sofia Scicolone, a woman burst out of the crowd, screaming blue-murder insults at her. Her father's wife!

The interview with LeRoy is a classic slice of Loren lore. 'Of course, my daughter canna spik Inglish,' said Romilda. 'Can you speak English?' said LeRoy. *'Che cosa dice, Mamma?'*/'What's he say, Mamma?' said Sophia. An Italian assistant went mad: 'How dare you tell lies to our director, he is very busy man, you cannot waste his time ...' Romilda took care of him, to the Magnani-manner born: 'We have come all the way from Naples. We have no money. We have not eaten for two days. We *must* work.' They got jobs.

On the set, they might easily have lost each other in the mystifying scrummage of extras by the thousand, and assistant-directors by the pack, except that, due to Romilda's inexperience, she had accepted a heavy bronze crown to wear. Very arduous, also very high; Sophia could not lose sight of it in the mêlée. For one scene, Sophia was placed close to the camera, Mamina having judiciously pointed out her daughter's photogenic qualities. Sophia also remembers the scene on-screen: out of focus behind Deborah Kerr.

'I invited two or three of my friends to see the film,' she recalls. '"Well, it's coming now," I'd say. Then: "Oh, where am I?" The focus was just on Deborah Kerr. It was, I think, a huge banquet scene. She was walking through thousands of people—and there I was looking around, trying to see where the camera was and I was just there, in front of it almost!'

They worked long nights and earned 21,000 lire, enough to rent a small furnished room on the Via Consenza. Life was really not much easier, yet everything seemed wonderful to the girl from the South with, although no one had yet told her, an atrocious Pozzuolian accent, which is even rougher on the ear than Napoli. Talk was not required from models, though, and soon the distinctly curvaceous teenager was hunting around for modelling jobs, and getting a few. Just a few. What little money she made, she kept wrapped in a handkerchief, under the mattress.

Apart from chasing Hollywood dollars at Cinecitta, the other top sport of post-war Italy was the beauty competition, which helped flood the reviving film industry with new faces and figures, and much

WHILE JIM WAS WITH THE CAPTAIN, PETER ROBERTS HURRIED ASHORE TO HIS SISTER'S HOTEL.

Great Scott! Diana—I thought you'd be on your way to England by now!

The police stopped me. They've heard I'm mixed up in this business at the café.

NOW THOROUGHLY SCARED, PETER PLEADED WITH DIANA TO TELL THE POLICE EVERYTHING SHE KNEW ...

Tell them I suggested framing Meg? You must be mad!

Right—stew in your own juice! I've had enough, Diana. I'm telling Jim everything I know.

PETER ROBERTS WAS AS GOOD AS HIS WORD. HE POURED OUT THE WHOLE STORY TO JIM.

Diana laid on the lot — the theft, the letters —everything! She even got Thompson to tip off Manuel you were coming—that's why you got the hot welcome from Alfredo.

Thanks, Roberts! The police will be glad to hear this.

AT THE CAFE, MEG'S MOTHER WATCHED OVER MEG TO MAKE SURE SHE HAD COMPLETELY RECOVERED FROM THE EFFECTS OF THE BLOW SHE'D RECEIVED IN THE RIOT.

My poor Meg, nothing seems to go right for you!

SUDDENLY RICARDO CORTEZ, MANUEL'S SON, BURST INTO THE ROOM ... TERRIFIED NOW, HE CONFESSED THAT HE HAD TAKEN THE MONEY FOR WHICH MEG HAD BEEN BLAMED ... MEG LISTENED IN ASTONISHMENT.

My father put me up to it. I was foolish—I thought it would mean the Lieutenant would go ... I love Meg. I did not know all this would happen.

Ricardo—how could you?

Well, thank goodness you've told the truth at last! Perhaps you know who killed Alice, too?

Yes! I know that ... But you must help me—they might kill me, too, if they knew I'd told anyone.

cheered up the populace and the newspapers. Sophia was invited to Cervia, all expenses paid for two, for the Queen of the Adriatic Sirens affair. She entered as Sofia Villani (her mother's name) and, although unplaced, was further invited to the finals at Salsomaggiore where she was selected Miss Elegance, in a swim-suit made by Mamina.

Beauty parades, though, were a brief episode in a month, or a year, a welcome break from the daily grind under the hot Roman sun searching dusty streets and offices for the more substantial work of modelling. Their first year was far from successful and Sophia remembers them being down to their last paltry 5,000 lire—enough to scuttle back to Pozzuoli if needs must. Romilda thought the time had come to call it quits towards the end of that year; now it was the daughter's determination which was the greater. She stuck at it. Even when Mamina went back to see Maria, nothing daunted Sophia from her purpose, which was not then to carve her own personal career in films, more simply to earn enough for herself and her mother—and to have Maria come and live with them in Rome.

The contests had their uses, as they led to modelling and that led to the *fumetti* magazines, love and adventure stories in photographic strip-cartoons, complete with dialogue bubbles or puffs of smoke: *fumetti*. At 10,000 lire a day, Sophia was soon excelling in the work; she became a special character known as The Vamp, a rôle never to be repeated, incidentally, in any form or fashion in her film rôles. She was told, however, she would get absolutely nowhere as Sofia Scicolone. Enter: Sofia Lazzaro ... something apparently connected with being beautiful enough to raise interest in dead men. A director called Giorgio Bianchi saw her work (and *fumetti* photos look very much like film-scene stills) and used her as an extra. One film led to another. She made seven in 1951, including *The Tuner Has Arrived* at the very un-princessly sum of 30,000 lire a day and her first credit in the record books as Sofia Lazzaro. Despite showing off much more, she had the same salary for *It's Him, Yes, Yes!* the first and, aside from later flashes, the last time she ever appeared bare-breasted on the screen. She did not want to strip—it was for the French version, the two directors insisted. 'I was hungry,' explained Sophia while Marilyn was saying much the same thing in Hollywood as her 1951 calendar shots came to front-page light. Loren enjoyed any notoriety far less than did Monroe, but neither revelation damaged the stars-to-be.

In Loren's case, the lack of clothes and the harem setting were coincidentally similar to that of her soon-to-be rival, Lollobrigida, in René Clair's *Les Belles de Nuit* around the same time. La Lollo,

though, kept her back to the camera throughout. Sophia was ordered very firmly to face front. 'I suffered an agony of embarrassment. I cannot bear being seen nearly naked even ... I am not exactly a tiny woman; when Sophia Loren is naked, this is a lot of nakedness. I drink to calm me. It does not put more clothes on me, but I blush less.'

One magazine cover led to another, and one beauty competition introduced Sofia Lazzaro to Carlo Ponti.

The Miss Rome contest was being staged at the Colle Oppio, an alfresco night club overlooking the Colosseum. Sophia was there with friends to watch the fun, nothing else. Ponti, a Milanese producer in partnership with Dino De Laurentiis and at the apex of the resurgent Rome film industry, was among the event's judges. He caught sight of Sophia and sent over an aide to suggest she took part in the proceedings. 'I looked at Ponti,' she remembers it well, very well. 'He seemed to have a pleasant face and I said yes. Actually, I think to myself: Sophia, if one of the judges suggests you enter—then you must win first prize.' She came second and got a contract instead; a backer, mentor, eventually a lover, and after the most tumultuous series of legal hassles, Vatican condemnation as public sinners, two weddings and one annulment, a husband as well.

After the prizes had been presented, Ponti invited the tall girl for a stroll through the park. He explained exactly who and what he was, that he had discovered stars like Lollobrigida, Valli, Rossi Drago, Bose, gave her a card and asked to see her at his office next day. Sophia, quite frankly, felt it was just another producer's line. 'Men,' she says of that time, 'when they approached me, it was only for one purpose. It was impossible for me to have men friends. They all only wished to be my lover. No! I started thinking about love very late.'

In his office, however, Ponti proved even more business-like ('He didn't look at me in the way that most men did') and with *The White Slave Trade* in mind, cinematically speaking, he signed her on the spot. She had the smallest of some 14 principal parts: a country girl straight off the farm and stuck, seduced and sold into big-city prostitution. One of her scenes lasted 90 seconds and shook them rigid in rushes—she faints at a dance and, carried into Silvana Pampanini's room, she admits to being pregnant. 'Mamma mia,' is the factoidal view accredited to some anonymous production man, 'she eats up Pampanini.' Her appetite had barely begun. Ponti was similarly impressed with the novice and called her back to his office and, so the story goes, offered a contract with Ponti–De Laurentiis, which Mamina refused out of hand. Supposedly, the two women—for such they now were—felt that Ponti's

Three Women. The indomitable Mamina, Romilda Villani, and her celebrated daughters: Sophia Loren and Maria Mussolini.

partner, the producer-husband of leading star Silvana Mangano, would hardly be keen on pushing Sophia's career as well as Mangano's. This same factoid then has Ponti countering, instead, with a personal contract with himself and keeping the pact secret from Dino De Laurentiis. Not so, says Sophia. 'I did not ever sign a contract with Carlo,' she told me. 'He said: "I, personally, am going to give you a certain amount of money each month and I am going to take care of you in the film business." So yes, it was always outside of Ponti–De Laurentiis; but no, I never signed anything.' In time, of course, this proved to be the best contract never signed in the cinema business.

'I have a feeling you could go far,' Ponti also told her. 'But it will not be what you think. It will be very hard work.' With that, he packed her off to Rome's

Experimental Centre of Cinematography Arts, to learn more about films and to do something about her accent, and he went shopping for work for her with other producers, until he found something suitable for her himself.

Goffredo Lombardo, chief of the Titanus combine, needed a girl who could swim for some fictional passages he was adding to a mass of underwater documentary footage. Sophia could not swim, did not tell anyone and, once shooting began, learned the hard way as *Woman of the Red Sea*. Lombardo took greater exception to the Lazzaro name than the slight deception about swimming. 'He decided a Scandinavian name would be more suitable for me. He thought of the Swedish actress Marta Toren ...' Lombardo went through the alphabet, Boren, Coren, Doren ... and Sophia Loren, 'ph' replacing the 'f',

17

was born, and received her first star billing in her first film (other than *Quo Vadis*) in colour.

Far more auspicious was *Aida*, although those in the know, Lollobrigida included, had backed off from it, regarding the assignment as something akin to an actor's graveyard: miming to operatic arias while covered from head to toe in black make-up. Loren's personality shone through the paint-job like an alarm-beacon on fire. The film was her first to reach America, where impresario Sol Hurok released it, and Stateside interest in the leading lady was rapid indeed—once it had been established (*a*) she was not an opera singer and (*b*) she was not really black. Even the immortal Cecil B. DeMille was quoted as exclaiming: 'Around this girl you could build something really super-colossal.'

Ponti's plan exactly. Viewing *Aida*, he realised he had much more than raw material on his books. 'I saw in Sophia a vitality, sensitivity and sense of rhythm that no Actors' Studio can teach. She was not an actress, she was an artist.' And worked like a Trojan: ten films during 1953, from *Carosello Napoletano*, which cued her first London visit and royal premiere the following year, to a touch more nudity as a comedy Cleopatra and co-starring status with Anthony Quinn in *Attila The Hun*. No one had a single complaint about her; everyone was impressed by Ponti's *brava figliola*, good kid.

She always knew her lines, and those of her fellow actors (which is not always the case of stars, let alone starlets), was never late or temperamental, and was fast gaining measurably in experience, confidence, style and maturity every way on every set. 'I'd finish one film on Saturday and start another on Monday. If British and American actresses had to work such hours as I did to make my name, they'd go on strike.'

The slog was worth it; Sophia was finding exactly what she had and how to use it, what she required to know and where to learn it. No longer was it merely a case of providing for the family—the career bug had bit. 'I will be a big star. I want everything that the big star has. I am not going to be poor any more.' Ponti, too, saw the shape of things to come and began masterminding the big build-up. 'Carlo saw that my body also had a heart and a brain and that with them I could achieve recognition as a serious actress. He shaped the development of my personality and tastes as well. Yet he never forced his ideas on me. He guided me indirectly, through suggestion.'

Slowly, their relationship was becoming more of a mutual respect and elation. Ponti, the producer and the man, had seen the blazing light about Loren. The body had soul.

The test came with *Gold of Naples*. The Ponti–De Laurentiis film was to be directed by Vittorio De Sica,

the latter-day matinée idol who helped create the *neo-realist* school of film-making after the war. De Sica would also star in one of the six sketches; Silvano Mangano took another; and a third-sketch heroine was a naughty Neapolitan pizza-seller called Sofia ... Ponti invited the director to meet Sophia in his office and De Sica conducted a film-test without cameras and was impressed as Ponti had hoped. 'You're a natural force,' De Sica told her when she suggested joining a drama school. 'Whatever you do is natural. Acting schools can't teach that, only inhibit it. You'll do many films and you'll learn as you go along. For you, it's the best way.'

She was kept in suspense about whether the rôle was hers for some weeks. What she did not know at the time was that De Laurentiis did not want her, he felt a bigger name was required. Ponti's hands were somewhat tied in pushing forward his discovery; De Sica's view carried the day. 'Take her then,' said Dino. 'But you'll regret it.' She was called the night before the company left for Naples, and walked —quite literally—away with her sketch and the film. If Sophia's recent nudity had put the more artificial Monroe in the Italian shade, so did her far more primitive walking motion—and her obvious flair for comedy. She did everything De Sica asked

Publicity. Sophia—who is she? Ponti knew and the world had to be made aware. Turn-on poses by the ton. Everything from Miss Weldor (sic) to pyjama-lounger.

of her and began to enter graduation class in the cinema. 'Respond,' he would say, 'with your entire body, not just your face and voice. Every bit of you must count. Including the tips of your little fingers.' When Sophia ambulated through the fake rain in Napoli as Sofia, *everything* counted. La Scicolone had returned home, a star in embryo. Grandfather Domenico was thrilled; Ponti's dreams were reinforced and the publicity machinery switched into top gear.

Even at this premature stage, Ponti had hopes way beyond mere success, Italian style. His eyes were on the glowing mecca of Hollywood. First, everyone had to know who Sophia Loren was. Enter Mario Natale, top Rome press agent, and the resultant flurry of pin-ups spread the joyous word in a language even far-off Hollywood could decipher. She went through the complete Monroe mill, turn-on poses by the thousands. Being lassooed by Indians, having bra adjusted by volunteer male hands, in fishnet tights with factory equipment as Miss Weldor (*sic*), the inevitable nude all but for a strategically placed bath towel, playing with a

highly phallic-looking eel, going to Mass—on one occasion holding her skirt so high on one magazine cover that the Italian *carabiniere* confiscated the entire edition and fined the publishers for an offence against public decency.

'Sex-appeal,' declared Sophia, 'is 50 per cent what you've got and 50 per cent what people think you've got. I think my eyes are best—the rest is up to others. I must try not to disillusion them.' She did not.

Editors and photographers clamoured for more, more; producers joined the frenzied queue. 'It requires Neapolitan slums to breed wildcats like Loren,' praised Joachim Bremer, film editor of West Germany's *Quick* magazine. No one really cared where she came from or how, they just wanted her to work for them. The film men had to wait, Ponti was arranging his set-piece for his star. He did not really have to search far for the idea. His partner, De Laurentiis, had made Mangano into a European idol and a mild American sensation with a film called *Bitter Rice*. Love in the paddy fields, *circa* 1947. Ponti took the same outline, give or take a comma, plumped for the same river Po setting, and had no less than six writers, including the fledgling Pasolini, knock it all into a shape befitting Loren's. They called it *Woman of the River*.

'Carlo never told me he was risking everything on me. If he had I would not have had the courage to get up in front of the cameras.' Her rôle sent her crashing through the entire gamut of possible emotions, passionate sensuality to distraught motherhood, and the cane-cutting locations led to still more thigh-thrashing pin-ups, plus a global distribution deal with Columbia, rapturous review headlines about Sophia the Sizzler—and a ring from Ponti to seal their partnership for life; secretly, until he could arrange his divorce.

Having proved his point—and Sophia's—Ponti then sat back and let the others have a chance. He was still chasing up the United States ('Look, she is more than just the beautiful body ... she is unique ... what you call the prototype') while she made her fourth film in 1954; four more followed in 1955, the year of Sophia as Italy called it, and Americans began to report it. She remembers the films better for what they brought her family. 'When you have got nothing and you start to earn some money, every job is a step forward, so every film meant new plans. After *Quo Vadis*, for instance, the first money I spent for my sister because she was very sick. From *Aida*, my mother got our first apartment, then something else and so on. What you want first is a house—I mean a house is a house; you have to have a house to feel that you have roots somewhere—then a car, furs, clothes and then jewels! When you learn that these things do not really mean anything for your happiness, you forget such superficialities and do in your life whatever you feel like doing. But when still very young you don't know and you like to spread around everything you can, if you can. It becomes an obsession. Even changing the colour of your hair. Every day! Because you are not sure of yourself, you're not secure and you don't really know what really counts in your life.'

Her mother was always a stable influence, financially. *Gold of Naples* meant a bigger apartment after three years cooped up in one room—'and Mamina and I did not have to cook in secret any more'. *River* meant Maria could finally come and join them in their four rooms and a terrace overlooking via Balzani, and *Too Bad She's Bad* paid for a better education for her sister.

On the artistic side, *Too Bad She's Bad* constituted the first teaming of Loren, Mastroianni and De Sica;

(Left and opposite page). Cheesecake. 'Sophia started out as a girl who was merely good to look at. I wish to stress that her beginnings were the same as scores of other actresses who just remain beautiful girls. Sophia has left them behind, achieving more than could have been hoped. She is the only film star who can speak her parts in four different languages (English, French, Spanish and Italian) without being dubbed. Sophia has really outclassed them all in breaking away from mere glamour ... I have followed her daily struggle and I love her for that, too.'—Carlo Ponti.

they had had separate sketches in *Our Times* and *The Sign of Venus*, which showed more of Loren the actress than the leggy toast of sex-appeal. *The Miller's Wife*, with Ponti back in the saddle, featured The Trio together again, and *Scandal in Sorrento* represented the fourth successive film with De Sica as co-star and counsellor—and the fruition of his prophecy. Sophia *did* improve each time out, and always shone particularly well when De Sica was in the cast. Of acting ability, comedy timing and, once again, style, he had plenty to offer and to teach. She also learned humility from him; never once did De Sica criticise or overrule orders of the directors of their films. For these assignments, like Loren, he was simply an actor.

The fact that they both hailed from Napoli was the secret of their vast *simpatico*. 'We understand each other so well as only Neapolitans can,' agreed Sophia. 'That's why it is so good to work with him. I have only to watch his face to know what he wants me to do. It is unusual to find such a rapport with anyone in this business.' She—they—had it with Mastroianni as well; he was born in Isola Litri, ten kilometres only from De Sica's birthplace of Sora. Like everyone else, Marcello was much taken with Sophia: 'She reminds me with great longing for the pleasure of my youth.'

From *The Sign of Venus*.

And De Sica was by now telling the world: 'Ah, Sophia! A young, unbroken filly so full of southern vitality. So unspoiled, so pliant. Her acting ability is not quite as fully developed as her physical presence. If it were we could announce a new Duse. We must wait for that.' Loren's legend has long since overtaken that of the *diva*, Duse.

Having already deposed La Pampanini and La Mangano, Loren's box-office kudos was by now impinging upon that of Gina Lollobrigida. In 1955, Sophia pushed her out of the headlines—and the queues—and with *Scandal in Sorrento* she took over a rôle La Lollo had played in two previous films with De Sica. That put paid to the entire Lollo battle, although even as late as 1965, Loren took up another vehicle Lollo had discarded: *Lady L.*

Continually stoked up by the wily press agent Natale, the Loren *v.* Lollo imbroglio was as choice a case of one-upmanship as anything Hollywood publicity men could have mustered. It first erupted in London when the two stars arrived and avoided each other like the plague while meeting the Queen at the 1954 Italian Film Festival. Fleet Street adored it. 'WHY LOLLO WAS MAD WITH ME' ran one Sunday paper headline quoting only Sophia's side of the feud. 'I wanted to be friendly with Gina ... Why not? It is true that my measurements excel Gina's but is that a reason why she should be so furious with me.'

Lollobrigida was one of four daughters of a Subiaco carpenter and had experienced the same kind of poverty-stricken childhood as Sophia and also started in films after *fumetti* work, in 1948. She tried to turn the hostilities into more of a class than sex war. 'Sophia is a *gran bella ragazza* (very pretty girl), but not the type to play a real lady. Not her fault ... just the way she looks.' But that was Sophia's argument: 'She is marvellous as a ragged peasant. She is always going to have trouble playing a *gran signora*, something I have no trouble doing.' The fact that she had not, up to that point, yet played a real lady on-screen did not seem to enter into it: she would—and she did. The European papers lapped it up and the American Press followed it through, blow by blow.

In retrospect, it was a most ingenious way to get Loren known in territories new, the U.S. in particular. Without Lollobrigida, though, it would never have worked as she was by far the better known at the time, more perhaps for her name, so funny to Anglo-Saxon ears (a positive gift for TV comics), than for her hour-glass figure. La Lollo was a handy—jolly—diminutive for headlines and thus she was the perfect bandwagon to leap upon. Loren *v.* Mangano, for instance, a positive fact in Rome, although Signora De Laurentiis was never much

enthused by a film career, would not have worked as well.

The culmination of the rumpus was Lollo pulling out of the third of the *Pane, Amore e .../Bread, Love and ...* series opposite De Sica. She moaned about money and vendettas but obviously wished to put the ragged peasant creation of those films far behind her; Sophia filled the vacancy with little hesitation. 'They wanted to call it *Pane, Amore e Donna Sofia* but I told them that would be too polemical.'

Years later, Loren added: 'I never took the rivalry seriously and I trust she didn't either.' Yet Lollo's career, including an even more disastrous Hollywood sojourn than Loren's, never fully recovered from backing out of the trumped-up brawl, still considered hot copy when *Newsweek* introduced Loren to America with a four-page movie-special headlined 'Italy's Sophia Loren, a new star—a "Mount Vesuvius"' on August 15, 1955. Ponti could not have afforded the space or the praise: 'Sophia is a monument difficult to ignore. A strapping 5 ft. 8 ins. in heelless Capezzios, she is four inches taller than the reigning Italian movie queen, Gina Lollobrigida. Her other dimensions—38–24–38—make Junoesque a pallid word. She has large, almond shaped golden eyes, spinnaker-full lips, a mop of honey-blonde (*sic*) hair and a way of moving that mobilises each one of her numerous other assets and puts them to work with a maximum of rhythmic efficiency.'

Ponti cabled Sophia: 'Learn English, you'll need it soon.' She mastered it inside three months, studying from 5–7 a.m. before work every morning with an Irishwoman who made her read poetry, especially T. S. Eliot. Ponti also went to work, reselling his protégée to the Americans. It was to be Hollywood or bust. 'An actress needs to have starred in American pictures,' ran the Ponti philosophy, 'in order to acquire an international reputation. In spite of her tremendous success, Bardot for instance remains a provincial actress in a way, because she never went to America and consequently her films are shown

Say *formaggio*! The teeth are fine but the eyes have it. The early films would hardly ever pan away from the remarkable bosom; then the Loren eyes, the most identifiable in the screen world, came into their own. The reason she abhors profile shots—'unflattering'—and has a prerequisite number of close-ups per film. Says Sophia: 'Eyes that have never cried can never be beautiful.' Except with a little help from her personal make-up man, Giuseppe (Pepito) Annunziata.

'If I could take only one cosmetic with me on a desert island,' she admits, 'it would be mascara.' For films, Pepito meets the upper lid's pencilling with a hair-fine line drawn along the lower lid, usually matching her costume colour with delicate eye-shadow. The mascara has to be waterproof—Sophia cries for real in her films.

only in specialised cinemas.'

Newsweek had mentioned that a company called King Bros. wanted Sophia for a film titled *An American Jubilee*. Nothing has been heard of either ever since. Ponti wanted something bigger and better for Loren. And he got it. Hollywood producer-director Stanley Kramer came shopping around for a European girl capable of the feminine lead in his expensive epic, *The Pride and the Passion*. Once in Rome, he could barely have missed hearing about Loren. If he did, Brando could have told him. Kramer wanted Brando in his film. Marlon did not like the script, but he tumbled, like everyone else, for Sophia. 'It's the damndest thing,' he said of her, 'when you see it you don't believe it. Then you look again ... and still you don't believe it.'

Kramer went off to see *Woman of the River* and, or so the story goes and it is too good to leave out here, his eyes lit up and, despite a heavy cold, he shot across to Ponti's office and snapped out an offer. 'I'll give her 200,000 dollars. Take it or leave it.' Ponti, nonplussed for perhaps the only time in his life, had been prepared for much less. 'I'll take it,' he gulped and Sophia joined the Kramer army, thundering through Spain like Napoleon's: 298 technicians, 46 vehicles, 1,500 head of cattle, Napoleonic and *guerrillero* extras numbering 9,400 at a con-

servative estimate, a far from happy Frank Sinatra in Brando's rôle, and Cary Grant. The Hollywood affair had begun in earnest.

Sinatra called her, as per norm, a gasser; Grant conquered her on their first meeting. 'Ah, yes, Miss Lorbridga ... er Brigloren ... I can never remember those Italian names!' Throughout the arduous location he remained at his most unassuming, tactful and generous. 'He was tireless in going over scenes with me, he corrected my faulty English and even built scenes in my favour. Without him I might have made a fool of myself.' Indeed there were soon solid-sounding rumours of impending nuptials. 'I knew he loved me and that if I chose to I could marry him,' Sophia has admitted. All her doubts on the matter faded, she reported in *Woman's Own*, when she realised they were too much alike and that mutual insecurity was no foundation for marriage. Grant still declared she had the wisdom of the ages in her soul. Yes, but did he want to marry her? 'Doesn't everybody?' was his best reply to that.

'I will not get married until I am 25.' This was Sophia in action for the international Press corps which arrived in force, continuing their Miss Sizzle commentaries as *Pride* got under way. The journalistic emphasis was still geared to the bosom, now proclaimed to be 39 inches, and Loren was tiring of the sport. Cheesecake, she told them, was fine and

necessary in the beginning, to attract attention, now she was trying to develop her acting. The marital queries flowed on. 'I want a husband who is ugly. I have a Neapolitan temperament. If I had a husband who is good-looking, he would attract other women and I would get jealous.' And her favourite actresses, please? Dietrich, Garbo, Bergman, Magnani!

The shooting dragged on—and on. Ponti began lining up other American propositions in Europe, while in Hollywood Anna Magnani won the Oscar for *The Rose Tattoo* (1955). Loren, ever honest, said she deplored the rôle and the film. 'No Italian woman should depict an Italian woman like that!' The *Daily Express*, meantime, suggested Magnani be named

Mother of the Italian cinema with Lollo and Loren as Hon. Daughters; and this, despite Magnani calling Lollo 'a living warning of the terrible things that can happen from over-inflation', and Loren 'a Neapolitan giraffe'. A new feud seemed to be in the making.

From Spain, Sophia dashed to Greece to make her delicious dive into the Aegean for *Boy on a Dolphin*. The drenched-dress shots of her flashed around the world and the film was rushed out to be first of her dollar-backed projects into general-release theatres. But it was no great shakes of a movie apart from Sophia's physique and she recalls with disdain having to stand in holes and ditches for half the

picture to avoid towering over her tiny co-star, Alan Ladd. No ditches were necessary in Libya where John Wayne had an inch or two of toupee to spare above her in *Legend of the Lost*, a Sahara Western. Sophia took another alfresco shower—'it seems I spent my first five years in the movies having people throw pails of water over me'—but a stubborn donkey obliterated the view and probably gave rise to the celebrated expression of 'Move your ass'.

Ponti, now in partnership with Marcello Girosi, producer of *Scandal in Sorrento*, had signed a two million dollar contract with Paramount. Hollywood was in the bag. Next stop: the Bougainvillaea-covered Bel Air home of Charles Vidor, where Sophia and Ponti lived together, and the real Hollywood chapter began. Up to now, Ponti had been playing at Hollywood like Monopoly. Now the factory got hold of his protégée and consequently the visit did not break records, nor make her a lasting star. She was in the right place at the wrong time. As usual, the Americans, clinging to fusty tradition like babies to the bottle, did not know how to deal with such foreign vibrancy, except to regulate and control (i.e. change) it. Cary Grant, alone, realised her comedy potential in *Houseboat*; Melville Shavelson and Sidney Lumet (on *That Kind of Woman*, made in New York incidentally) were the sole directors man enough to let her go, flow. As for the rest, from *Black Orchid* to the compulsory Western, *Heller in Pink Tights* (much less a cliché under Cukor), they were mendacious come-ons, with a succession of leading men which, as *Time* maga-

Meet Sophia! George Raft found she was 'Mount Vesuvius, Etna and Krakatoa, all in one,' so everyone wanted to look. The reception for *The Pride and The Passion* was packed; big John Wayne kept guard over her for his *Legend of The Lost* party. In Italy, it was Carlo Ponti's turn to host his wife's *Marriage, Italian Style* with Mastroianni; and the only place they found they could film in (relative) peace was in Russia with Ludmila Savalyeva as guide during *Sunflower*. No affair, however, could ever match the welcome-to-Hollywood blast in 1957 when Jayne Mansfield fell out of her dress.

zine ruefully pointed out, she could have swallowed given half a glass of water.

'I had the chance to work with the greatest actors, starting with Cary Grant; I have worked with almost all of them: John Wayne, William Holden, Clark Gable, Paul Newman. But it is very difficult for me to get the right partner. I think the only right one, beside Richard Burton recently, was Marcello Mastroianni and also Peter O'Toole. I think Peter is right for me on the screen, but of course *Man of La Mancha* was not the right film because we did not have a lot to do together.'

She never floundered, it is true, though Hollywood did its routine best/worst to stifle something unique into the normal faceless, graceless factory-line enamel varnishing. Loren took more from the experience than was ever doled out; her firmest grounding in artistic and professional survival which later allowed her to accomplish that which no

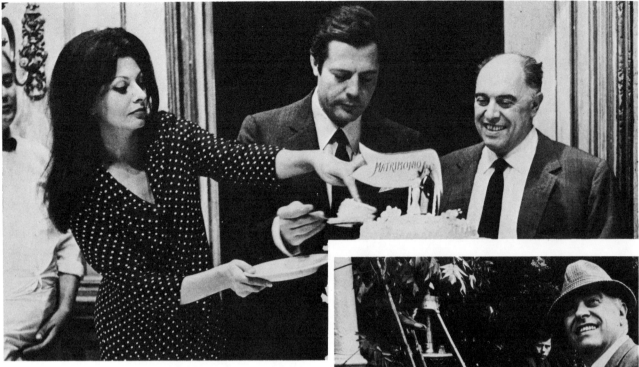

foreign actor has managed, before or since: to return home and become a bigger international name than she had even been in Hollywood. On her own time, terms and turf. A stupendous achievement.

The film-city welcoming party should have signalled the mess she had joined. The invitation list for the big Paramount pour covered anyone who was (which meant: is) anyone, including Jayne Mansfield. Having already done her horizontal and pneumatic best to shake, rattle and roll poor Marilyn Monroe, Jayne attempted to heave Loren out of her own reception's limelight. She stalked the table which Sophia was sharing with a friend from *Dolphin*, Clifton Webb, crept up behind her, bending low for the photographic phalanx, so much so that her right breast cascaded out of her low-cut gown. 'Gee!' squeaked Jayne, 'I was only trying to be friendly!' This was still mild 1957, so the pictures could hardly be splashed across the nation's breakfast. Once again, Loren (whose face at the exposure was a treat!) won the day. She was a lady and Jayne ... well, the breast (surprisingly) was not as big as the boob.

The vital Hollywood début was a tough item: Eugene O'Neill's *Desire Under the Elms*. On paper it seemed too much too expect of any tongue new to the vagaries of English, but no (the one word she had difficulty in pronouncing), Loren handled herself superbly. She made the tragic Anna glow and never lost a scene in the clinches between the shallow Anthony Perkins and an even more mis-cast Burl Ives. She shone infinitely better in *Houseboat*, which Cary Grant originally had ordered for his then-wife, Betsy Drake.

The Pontis. Sophia and Carlo. 'You would only have to see us on a Sunday to realise how basically normal we are.

The true cause of Sophia's radiance was not the re-tailored script, however, but a phone call on September 17, 1957. 'You were married an hour ago,' said the know-all voice of Louella Parsons. 'You are now Mrs. Ponti.' For even that particular Hollywood gossip-hen, it must have been a rarity to know a star was wed before the star knew it. The ceremony had taken place in Juarez, Mexico, with two lawyers standing in for the couple—straight after Ponti's divorce, also by proxy, from his wife since 1946, Giuliana Fiastri, an army general's daughter and the mother of Ponti's two children.

The sheer bliss of attaining legal sanction at last for her love—'Carlo is my life! Everything else I have is expendable. I want seven children!'—was to be short-lived and lead them up, down and back up a murky road of Vatican pontification, bigamy charges, annulment, French citizenship, re-divorce and re-marriage, which in turn would take some toll, slight but noticeable, of the actress's continuing sparkle and quality of output.

Sophia had completed only two of her five Los Angeles commitments, when against her new hus-band's wishes she quit for London to make *The Key* for Carl Foreman—and ran directly into the first blast of cold indignation from the Vatican which refused to recognise the Mexican divorce. Excommunication from the Catholic Church was threatened by an attorney of the Vatican Rota tribunal, writing in *L'Osservatore della Domenica* and referring to 'a young, beautiful Italian film actress'. The Rota, breathed the article's hellfire and brimstone, could never admit that 'concubinage should be called marriage'.

The Italian Men's Catholic Action group urged all Catholics to shun Loren films and—to avoid a head-long confrontation—the Pontis stayed well away from Italy, working and living in America, Britain or Switzerland, until they felt the situation had cooled. She was, though, still castigated as a public sinner when she became godmother to her sister's daughter in 1963; Maria had married Romano Mussolini, jazz-pianist son of Il Duce, in March, 1962.

By strange coincidence, it was when Sophia was about to make another war film for Foreman, *The Victors* in 1963, that the Pontis were charged with bigamy by a member of the Italian public—not the ex-Mrs. Ponti (Sophia said she might have understood that) but a certain Signora Brambilla, whom

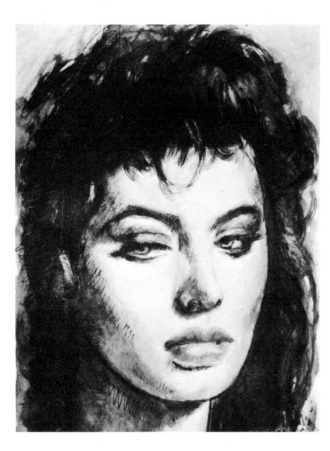

they had never met, nor, apparently, harmed. Loren withdrew from the film (replaced by Rossano Schiaffino; like all her other rivals, long since forgotten) and, faced with a possible jail term, they had the Mexican marriage annulled and took up French residency in order to marry anew.

'I give up,' exclaimed Sophia angrily from time to time, wearing her ring and, naturally, still living with Ponti. 'I'm married, I'm not married. I'm this, I'm that. Basta! I feel married and lots of married people don't feel married.' In 1965, a French court granted Ponti a second divorce from Giuliana and he was married once more to his Sophia by the Mayor of Sèvres, Dr. Charles Odie, outside Paris on April 9, 1966. Two years later, an Italian appellate court dismissed all bigamy charges.

The Key had proved a better critical and artistic success than most of her Hollywood films clubbed together. Foreman felt Sophia would be eventually as great as Garbo, and Trevor Howard, not one known for fulsome praise, was exceedingly impressed. 'That's a real working woman. Not like those teenage tots who think once they've been in a picture they're too important to be gracious to their colleagues by being on time.' William Holden (instead of Henry Fonda) was the co-lead, and quickly planned a reprise of the partnership in a venture called *Blaze to the Sun*, to have been directed by John Huston. Nothing came of the plan, how-

ever; nor of the George Cukor idea of *The American Girl and a Man*. Other films Loren had been named for included *A Shot in the Dark*, second of the Peter Sellers-Insp. Clouseau farces, which Elke Sommer took over, and two other British productions both to suffer from the non-talent of Kim Novak: *Of Human Bondage* and *Moll Flanders*.

Sophia had been quick to recognise that Stella in *The Key* was a meaty woman's rôle, and other than hearing that if she could not make it Ingrid Bergman probably would, what attracted Sophia even more to the production was Foreman's interest in her acting, not her figure; this befitted her horizons and her newly married status. 'Five years ago,' she told the British papers sardonically, 'they said I was hopeless: my mouth was too wide, my eyes too dark, my nose too long. Now I am known and rich—so my mouth is suddenly fine, my eyes are attractive, and my nose is bewitching! More important, today I am a woman. Yesterday I was a girl. Good for nothing but pin-ups. Women disliked me and they were right. Their husbands came away from my films leering. I would hate it if my husband did that.'

In 1958, she returned to Hollywood to complete her contracts: only *That Kind of Woman* could be considered memorable of the three films involved. None of the ritzy Cadillacs, fancy chauffeurs, lavish cottages and other film city impedimenta could make up for the kind of vehicles supposedly designed with Loren in mind; most times, instead of riding clear to glory, she had to get out and push. Mistakes, she termed them later, though never did she sneer at her Hollywood adventure. No, not very good, Ponti would agree—although he had set up most of them. They were, though, not *that* bad for Hollywood in the late '50s, and more impressive than anything facing Lollobrigida on her arrival as soon as Sophia left town. The films served their major purpose: making Loren a name from coast to coast. She need never work there again, and thus far she has not.

'I shall regard my Hollywood days very highly always,' Sophia says today, 'and I am quite willing to return for a good script. My time there was a great experience for me. I had the chance to do many, many films, work with many important directors and the greatest actors—a wonderful school for me. If it is an experience it is always good, even if sometimes it does not turn out right, it can still be a positive experience if you learn from it. And I would never have become ... not famous, let's say, known ... if I had not gone to America. If I had stayed in my country, I would have been a very well-known Italian actress today and that is all.'

Back in her beloved Napoli, she showed Los Angeles exactly what it was missing—and had missed—when she returned to the wonderfully zesty kind of Neapolitan marvel she had been before—in *It Started in Naples*, Clark Gable's penultimate movie. *A Breath of Scandal* (in Austria) did not work at all and *The Millionairess* (in London) did, perhaps, more for Peter Sellers than Loren. She looked fantastic, positively eatable—even in her scenes with De Sica, the morning after losing £250,000 worth of jewellery in a burglary. To Sophia, the robbery was like rape. Ever since *Gold of Naples*, Ponti had celebrated each new premiere with a piece of jewellery, and although priceless in value, the collection was much more sentimental to her. 'Each piece evokes some memory of my life with Carlo and at the same time reassured me that I could never go hungry again.'

The theft took place while she was driving to the airport to meet Ponti. In the event, he had something to stop the next day's tears ... *Two Women*. In 1957, Italy's leading novelist, Alberto Moravia, had written his book *La Ciociara*, an indomitable saga of a widowed mother and teenage daughter on the run from the war in Italy. Ponti snapped up the rights and like everyone else—De Sica the chosen director included—felt Anna Magnani was the perfect choice as the mother, with Loren as the 17-year-old daughter. Everyone agreed, except, that is, the

fiery Magnani. 'I'm too young to play Loren's mother,' she howled at De Sica. (She was 52; Loren's Mamina, 47.) 'Let her play the part herself.' Her derisive screams had De Sica recalling one particular sequence he loved in *Desire Under the Elms*: where Loren tells Perkins she has killed their child to prove her love for him. The more De Sica pondered, the more he felt his young protégée could handle *La Ciociara*. As for Sophia, it was like asking her to try and talk for 90 minutes about her childhood. 'Not since *Gold of Naples* had I felt such a total identification with a rôle. I had lived through the real thing with my mother, whose character resembles La Ciociara. The gestures, the language, the attitudes came to me as naturally as breathing.'

So did the awards. The gamble, if such it had ever really been, came off in spades. Sophia was the best actress at the 1961 Cannes and Cork festivals, and won the British Film Academy and the New York Film Critics' trophies. When she was nominated for an Oscar the following year, her first intention was to fly to the ceremony. 'Imagine, if an Italian girl gets an Oscar for an Italian picture and suppose I'm not there.' *Time* magazine said she would be and welcomed her with a cover story on April 6, 1962; at least in *Time*-style it was regarded as a welcome: 'Her feet are too big. Her nose is too long. Her teeth are uneven. She has the neck, as one of her rivals has put it, of "a Neapolitan giraffe". Her waist seems to

Mentor. 'You are a natural force. Respond with your entire body. Every bit of you must count. Including the tips of your little fingers.' Vittorio De Sica's instructions to Loren during *Gold of Naples*, 1954; since when he had made 14 films with her as co-star or director. (Above) *Too Bad, She's Bad*; (above, right) *Sunflower* in Moscow; (right) *The Voyage* in Palermo in the winter of '73.

begin in the middle of her thighs, and she has big, half-bushel hips. She runs like a fullback. Her hands are huge. Her forehead is low. Her mouth is too large. And *mamma mia*, she is absolutely gorgeous.'

Sophia got cold feet. More nerves than the other nominees: Audrey Hepburn, *Breakfast at Tiffany's*; Piper Laurie, *The Hustler*; Geraldine Page, *Summer and Smoke*; and Natalie Wood, *Splendour in the Grass*. 'If I won,' she said, 'I would faint and I prefer to faint at home.' April 9 was the longest night of that year as Sophia and Carlo waited for news. 'It's stupid to hope,' she kept repeating. 'Yes,' nodded Ponti, 'they've never given it to anybody in a foreign film.' In 1962, they did not have much choice. The phone jangled. It was Cary Grant in Hollywood. The Oscar was Sophia's. To join Ponti's for *La Strada*, the first ever officially presented to a foreign film (in 1956). Together, the Pontis, again with De Sica and Mastroianni, would make a third Oscar possible for *Yesterday, Today and Tomorrow*.

35

The immediate post-Oscar days passed, Sophia has said, in an ecstatic blur. 'I vaguely remember telegraph boys delivering bundles of messages from every corner of the globe, reporters and cameramen over-running the apartment, champagne popping. At the end, exhausted, I lay on my bed between Mamina and Maria. We had no need of words. We knew we were all thinking of our first home in Pozzuoli and the distance we had travelled.'

The journey was far from over ... After the mammoth *El Cid* and more Napoli-like fun and games in *Madame* and *Boccaccio '70*, the ride got a trifle bumpy, with *Five Miles to Midnight* in France (Loren had matured, Anthony Perkins had not); and perhaps the sole flop of the Loren–De Sica films, *The Condemned of Altona*: some very heavy meat from Sartre which proved no less tough when delivered to the cinematic table as Loren's 50th picture. Yet a full million dollars was proffered for *The Fall of the Roman Empire* and the pace settled into joyous bliss with a double teaming of Loren, Mastroianni and De Sica, in *Yesterday, Today and Tomorrow* in 1963 and *Marriage, Italian Style*, 1964.

While Mastroianni and director Pietro Germi (one of

Partner. 'My favourite leading lady? Ah! Sophia without a doubt. She is so warm, so lovely, so ... *Italian!*' Marcello Mastroianni, like De Sica, appeared with Sophia (in separate yarns) in *Tempi Nostri*, 1953. The Trio officially formed the following year in *Too Bad, She's Bad*—first of seven outings for Sophia and 'my husband!' (Above) *Lucky To Be A Woman*; (right) *Sunflower*.

the few leading Italian directors Sophia has never worked with) actually began the *all'italiana* style of title in 1961 with *Divorce, Italian Style*, it was the re-teaming of Sophia and Marcello which put the expression on the map. Within months of their *Marriage*, all Italy was copying the logo. Apart from those companies still immersed into ripping-off the other going genres, the Bond-type sagas numbered anything from 001 to 008, and the various 'spaghetti-Westerns' fashioned after director Sergio Leone, there was a Roman proliferation of Lorenish handles: *War, Italian Style* (with Buster Keaton of all people); *Menage, Italian Style*; *Adultery, Italian Style*; *Caprice, Italian Style*; and foreign distributors did not help matters by adding the suffix to almost anything emanating from Italy. But then as

De Sica, who hated his own film's title, says: distributors never have any taste.

Marcello Mastroianni has proved to be the most perfect foil for Loren—comedienne or tragedienne—reminiscent, in fact, of the old-time Hollywood duos. Since their early films together, Mastroianni had climbed to similar heady heights in the company of Visconti, Antonioni and in the two most hailed films of Fellini, *La Dolce Vita* and $8\frac{1}{2}$. As before, there was no rivalry in their teamship and in 1964 they were written of as the hottest twosome in front of any movie camera anywhere.

Donald Zec, of the *Daily Mirror*, put it all down to Formula X, the kind of magic chemistry that flares only between very special people and saves a lot of space in trying to delineate more fully their charm. Sophia told Zec: 'Marcello is a man who thinks like a man, talks like a man—is a man. He has so much magnetism, he brings out the very soul in a woman.' Marcello likewise said: 'There is a woman who thinks like a woman, talks like a woman, behaves like a woman—never a star. We communicate with each other by instinct. With her I do not need to labour. It is like a meeting of two souls. Ah! she is honest, she is tranquil.'

The truth was they were not so much opposite, fusing as one, as very much the same single entity; if they ever wanted to change sex, they would want to be each other. They are the missing parts of a puzzle, each commanding the respect and attention of the other, each able to take the upper or lower berth in the battle, or the enjoining, of the sexes. They are, in a word: Italy, male and female. Their *Marriage* being the definitive case in point.

There are several anecdotes about Sophia returning home to Naples, for locations and otherwise, bringing wedding presents for former school-friends who never knew she knew about their marriages, and so on. None more typifies Sophia's everlasting success as *la donna* (or indeed, *la diva*) *popolana*, than her short location work in a Naples prison for the first of the *Yesterday, Today and Tomorrow* sketches, about the wife getting pregnant every year to stay out of jail. A prisoner passed a poem to De Sica and he read it to the unit. 'May God bring a real baby to bless the life of a certain lovely lady,' it began ... Sophia broke down and fled the set in tears. Only Ponti knew, but Sophia was pregnant again, after several earlier miscarriages. Her followers wished her motherhood as much as she and Carlo did. She took some time off before shooting the Moravia episode in a Rolls in Milan and suddenly felt 'something awful happening'. She lost another child—though, professional to the last, who would know it on viewing the last episode of that trio, as the brightly cheerful, simply gorgeous call-girl, Mara. It is, all the same, a film Sophia Loren did not enjoy watching, for some years.

Her constitution, however, remains enormous. Compared to other superstars, Liz Taylor for example, as well known for illnesses as husbands, Sophia is almost arrogantly healthy. She contracted pneumonia when being continually soaked in *Gold of Naples*, but has rarely held up production through ill-health and never through temperament. When she does suffer from fatigue, she usually breaks something—her collar bone towards the end of *El Cid*, for instance. Otherwise her shooting schedule is the same as it has been throughout 67 films in 25 years: studying lines at 6 a.m., make-up and on the set by 9 a.m., shooting to 6 p.m. or even 8.30 p.m. 'To me,' she has explained, 'acting is like painting to an artist or composing to a musician—the only way of self-expression. I must study a part and try to feel it. I am nervous when I am angry with myself, when I make a mistake or talk too much. I am not one who can laugh or cry just when they tell me. When acting, I feel courageous, secure, creative, more truly alive.'

The next batch of scatter-shot films saw something of a marked run-down of the glories of the immediate past: very much connected with the looming bigamy charge keeping both Pontis out of Italy. *Operation Crossbow* in London provided little more than an unimportant cameo in a war saga; *Lady L* in Switzerland, France and London was a full-blown epic, or should have been until M.G.M. changed its mind, and the released version suffered acutely from heavy time-scissoring. *Judith* took Sophia to Israel in 1966 and saw a welcome return of those flashing legs and thighs, but very little else, not even good propaganda; and *Arabesque*, though polished to gleam, was a watered-down version of Stanley Donen's earlier *Charade* thriller. As always, there was something bright on the horizon. The return of Charlie Chaplin, no less, with *A Countess from Hong Kong*.

Sometime after *Boccaccio '70*, Ponti had suggested a sequel, with Charlie Chaplin directing one Loren episode. The hope was not exactly wasted on anyone—Chaplin included. A friend told Sophia a few years later that Chaplin indeed knew her work and wanted to make a film with her. 'He was very impressed when he saw me in *Yesterday, Today and Tomorrow* and thought about a project he had in

his drawer that he had planned to do long before with Paulette Goddard.' She heard nothing direct from the grand old man—'for mé the supreme genius of film, practically the inventor of the art'—until filming *Lady L* near Vevey, where the Chaplin Swiss family mansion is ensconced. Sophia was invited to dinner.

Chaplin met her at the door and Sophia vividly remembers she 'blushed with excitement and, incredibly, so did he. Almost at once, he plunged into the script, a high comedy about an American diplomat and a wild Russian princess. As he acted it out, the years fell from him like a cloth. He still has the litheness, the grace of a young dancer. Enthralled, I watched the swift movements of his body, how he used his hands and feet, the vitality and eloquence of his eyes and mouth ... After dinner, he described his own humble beginnings, sensing I think, that it would bring us closer together.'

Hopes were high during shooting at Pinewood studios. If ever everyone in movies wished a picture to succeed, this was it. The film, alas, let everyone down. Faced with such a monumental flop, critics hit back as if they had been conned. Reviews blasted Chaplin's senility, and Marlon Brando, finally co-starring with Loren after all, did not get nor deserve any better. Sophia alone, save for Patrick Cargill, emerged with honour intact. Yet again, she had been presented with a vehicle she had to push—up a steep hill. She defends it as a warm memory.

'It was a graceful film, it really had all the grace that only Charlie Chaplin could have put in. Of course, it was not a *chef d'œuvre* but it was charming—and did not deserve what was said about it. I would hope that it will one day soon be rediscovered, because it has been a happy moment of my life.'

Some salve for recent wounds came in two Italian productions, almost quickies again, for Ponti: the exquisite *Cinderella, Italian Style* with Omar Sharif, 1967, and *Ghosts, Italian Style*, far less successful under the veteran director Renato Castellani. Both lacked the essential touch of De Sica (once hailed in the States as master of the unwashed soap-opera) and the impact of Mastroianni's presence.

For once, however, neither Loren nor Ponti was studying the returns. Their ultimate production was in store as Italy's *Cinderella* went into semi-retirement, in a determined effort to make sure her latest pregnancy would not fail. Losing her last baby at five months, she said, had been the most vital thing that had happened to her: 'a woman is born to be a mother and a mother I will be'. Under the expert care and guidance of Swiss gynaecologist Dr. Hubert de Watteville, the plan was to spend the majority of the pregnancy in bed for 20 hours a day, right up to labour and delivery. Ponti rented an apartment for

Finale? The seventh Loren–Mastroianni teaming: *The Priest's Wife*, 1970.

Motherhood. She kept playing mothers, like the over-fertile Adelina in *Yesterday, Today and Tomorrow* (right), yet seemed fated to be denied true maternal bliss with an agonising succession of miscarriages. Until 1968, half a year or more of literal confinement in Geneva and the birth of Carlo Jr., or Chippy (above) on December 29. At last Sophia had her own baby to feed. Four years and nine days later, his brother Eduardo, or Dodo, arrived (left). 'It is the very best thing a woman can do—to have a child.'

her, £45 a day, at the Geneva Inter-Continental hotel, where the room temperature was kept to a strictly constant 68–70 degrees. And this time—gloriously—it worked. Carlo Ponti Jr., was born three weeks early by Caesarian section on December 29, 1968. The proud mother received more cables than when she won the Oscar. *La mamma popolana!* Her ecstasy was shown to the world at a Press conference in Geneva, Sophia looking scared when first wheeled into the room, still in her bed. 'I *was* frightened ... having had this great experience and having stayed for such a long time from the world.' Chippy's next appearance (the nickname derives from his initials, CPJr.) was in his mother's come-back, *Sunflower*, another typically bold Ponti venture—the first Italian film with locations inside a very co-operative Russia. Ponti was already into negotiations in Moscow to bring off Sophia's major screen ambition, *Anna Karenina* for, perhaps, Visconti. (The project is now being considered as a highly expensive serial for television, after her *Brief Encounter* re-make for TV.)

De Sica and Mastroianni were back on the team; therefore, all boded well. 'She has confidence in me,' the director once explained their success. 'She does not read the script first. I read it, then run through, with her. That way, I, too, get the sense, not of the meaning—of the ballet. Acting is music to me.' Their latest symphony was incorrectly orchestrated for the pop age. Often an idyllic U.S.S.R. travelogue, with Sophia, exceptionally divine and distraught, searching the Ukraine for her lost Italian soldier husband, *Sunflower* was as much out of date, out of true with the current film climate—despite an over-publicised bigamy angle—as Chaplin's *Countess* had been.

Ever-flexible, Ponti soldiered on, starred Sophia and Marcello for the seventh time in his Champion company's satirical punch at the Vatican: *The Married Priest*—only to make up for it a year later by having Loren become a nun in *White Sister*. The Pontis also went back to New York for *Lady Liberty*—an Italian film made their way, nothing American but about things American—and before the end of her musical epic, *Man of La Mancha*, good news was out again. Sophia was pregnant once more and Dr. de Watteville took over her career until after Eduardo (Dodo) Ponti arrived on January 6, 1973.

'I went through so much to have these children that I would give up working for them—if I had to be far away from them.' She never was; it was Palermo, Sicily, in *The Voyage*, out of Pirandello by De Sica, with Richard Burton; Paris and Lyons for her newest French venture, *The Verdict* for director André Cayatte. Jean Gabin, in what he has firmly declared to be his farewell rôle, is the veteran judge interceded with by Loren whose son is accused of murder. Sophia, however, shows no sign, nor desire, for retirement. 'If I stopped right now I would feel like my arm was cut off. However ... fame and a career could never take the place of love and a family. Fame is here today and then tomorrow it may forget your name. The family remains.'

Cinderella has all the golden slipper she needs, being mother now as well as wife and actress. For Sophia Loren, motherhood was the ultimate state of normalcy that she craved for during a dozen years or more. In his analytical interview with her for America's *Show* magazine in 1962, Alberto Moravia continually probed for her meaning of the word she used so often: normal. Noting her need for success to counter-balance the psychological abnormalities of her youth without a father, he pointed out a bitter nexus between the two normalities in her life: career and marriage from the same provider.

Moravia reminded her how her drive toward a normal family had been blocked because her parents were unmarried, just as the fact that Ponti had been married originally blocked her drive to a normal married life. What was this famous normalcy she sought? Simply a desire to be like other women which was in complete contradiction with her ambition as an actress that made her utterly different from other women—'not just rare, but unique'. At the same time, the novelist agreed that if her private life had been normal, she might have lacked any spur to attain the abnormalities of her career.

Loren later told Moravia that he was attaching too much importance to the feeling of abnormality; and maybe he was, in pursuance of a good story. Yet in the same magazine, Ponti himself was writing about life with Loren. 'We are freaks ... An actress and a producer are nothing but freaks. Not by notice, but by implication. That is what people want us to be. Actually our great ambition is to be like them, indistinguishable ... you would only have to see us on a Sunday to realise how basically normal we are ... It is our fault if our lives are what they are, nobody else's.'

For her part, Sophia describes her life today as very tranquil; and she does, it is true, glow with positive serenity. 'My face is my mirror,' she told me. 'If I am not fine, if I have problems, you can tell it right away. But I am quite rational in what I do. I don't do crazy things—well, it is rare, very rare; it can happen sometimes! I have found an equilibrium in my life and I am quite satisfied with what I have got.

'I am still very much excited about working, too. I like the films they make nowadays: they dare much more than they used to. Sometimes they exaggerate because there are still certain things that cannot be

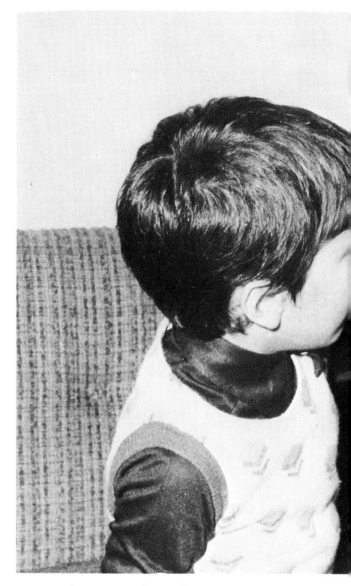

seen on the screen. Generally, most of the things they do I am always interested in seeing—except the vulgarity. When they push too much and become vulgarly destructive, this I cannot stand. If they asked me to do things like that, then I think I would quit. Quietly. No press conference announcing a last film. No, no, I would just retire, steal away. It's the best way because if by any chance after two or three years something interesting comes up, I would not —like Sinatra—have to say, "Well, you know, I've thought it over and decided to come back."'

Immediate future plans include two more films with De Sica in Naples, *La Maga*, 'a wild comedy' and a World War II drama, tentatively titled *Vesuvius*; plus the re-make of *Brief Encounter* set for London. 'I will go on, maybe one film a year; two, three or none. It depends. If I feel something is right for me at that moment, then I will do it. I feel much more at home—more confident—if it is a project that my husband and I have talked over and worked at to-

Triumphant. Chippy, Dodo and Mama.

gether. Otherwise I am a little unhappy ... sometimes, you make a mistake. But that's our profession —every profession, no? If people were 100 per cent every time they started something, it would be too easy. And also very boring.'

Sophia Loren—so full, so fine, so fiery, *so* freaky! —has steered the eccentricities, vicissitudes, narcissitudes, dangers, deceits and resounding prat-falls of an international screen career with greater lasting merit and love (on both sides of the camera) than many of her contemporary fellow freaks. Throughout, she has stayed exceedingly true to herself, her dreams and realities—especially to her audience. The provocative personification of body and soul, she delivers still her promises, sets sights still on high, and once achieving them, searches for vistas even higher. 'I would like to do something very highly dramatical, but really push at the extremes of tragedy. But who could do it? Visconti—ten years ago he was right. Cacoyannis—he did it already. Maybe Buñuel: I like

the strange things he does, not so much *Belle de Jour* as *Viridiana*—that kind of atmosphere. And, of course, now I am mad about Ingmar Bergman after *Cries and Whispers*. I just flipped over that!' Bergman and Loren: a confrontation devoutly to be wished.

Like the rest of us, admiring in the cinema, she is more content than happy with life, loving and meeting it, on the screen and off, in the simplest, most essential and joyous of attitudes. She is Neapolitan, therefore philosophic. 'There is enough life in me to be actress, lover and mother all at once. As long as the public is not tired of me, I will go on working. When it is over, I will say *ciao* and *grazie* and then I retire.' Not yet. Not just yet. Fame was rightly hers yesterday, remains so today, and tomorrow will not forget her name for generations to come.

Epic début. Cinecitta, 1950, and hordes gathered to play hordes in *Quo Vadis*, Sofia Scicolone among them: somewhere.

The extra and fledgling films of Sophia Scicolone/Lazzaro/Loren

Or the lost films of … The majority of Loren filmographies begin with *Aida*, even *Gold of Naples*, several miss out *Tempi Nostri* completely, and the order of her feature-films up to the first dollar-backed projects is often woefully inaccurate. Understandable; even with so contemporary a legend as Loren's, the detection employed in resurrecting examples of her earliest work as a Rome extra and raw starlet is by no means simple. How, for instance, do you locate a 15-year-old from Pozzuoli searching for Mamma's tall crown in the *Quo Vadis* crowd scenes? You could go blind! However, with the grateful assistance of the immaculately compiled Annuario del Cinema Italiano year-books (which teach Britain a considerable lesson in the collation of films facts and figures); every screen researcher's friend, John Kobal; and by no means least, Ms. Loren herself—'as best my memory allows'—this initial listing of her first 25 films is as wholly accurate as possible. The actual order is determined by both the year of production (not release) and the Italian industry's official registration numbering system which began only in 1938 (with Goffredo Alessandrini's *Luciano Serra, Pilota* as No. 1). Sophia enters the lists at 847; her latest Italian venture, *The Voyage*, is 5679.

Credit-note: Distribution companies listed here, and in the major filmography section, are British only; aka. signifies: also known as.

As Sofia Scicolone, film extra

1950

QUO VADIS. American. M.G.M. *Director:* Mervyn LeRoy. *Producer:* Sam Zimbalist. *Script:* John Le Mahin, Sonya Livien, S. N. Behrman—*from the novel by* Henryk Sienkiewicz. *Photography:* Robert Surtees, William Skall. *Editor:* Ralph Winters. *Music:* Miklos Rozsa. *Art Directors:* William Horning, Cedric Gibbons, Edward Carfagno. *Historical Adviser:* Hugh Gray. *Choreography:* Marta Obolensky, Auriel Millos. Technicolor. 167 minutes.

Cast: Robert Taylor, Deborah Kerr, Leo Genn, Peter Ustinov, Patricia Laffan, Finlay Currie, Abraham Sofaer, Marina Berti, Buddy Bear, Felix Aylmer, Nora Swinburne, Ralph Truman.

Amid the multitudinous crowd scenes, Sofia Scicolone entering screen history with the most famous anecdote about an extra since David Niven joined Central Casting in Hollywood as Anglo-Saxon Type No. 2008. See Biography section, page 14.

CUORI SUL MARE/Hearts at Sea.
Italo-French. Cine-Albatros co-production.
Director: Giorgio Bianchi.
Cast: Jacques Sernas, Milly Vitale, Doris Dowling, Charles Vanel, Marina Berti.
[Registration number: 847]

IL VOTO/The Vote. Italian. A.R.A. Films Production. *Director:* Mario Bonnard.
Cast: Doris Duranti, Georgio De Lullo, M. G. Franchia, R. Murlo, L. Valenti, L. Billi. [No. 899]

LE SEI MOGLIE DI BARBARLU/Bluebeard's Seven Wives. Italian. Golden Film production. *Director:* Carlo Ludovico Bragaglia. 85 minutes.
Cast: Toto, Isa Barzizza, Luigi Pavese, C. Ninchi, A. Bragaglia, T. Buazzelli, M. Povena, M. Castellani. [No. 908]

IO SONO IL CAPATZ. Italian. Jolly Film production. *Director:* Giorgio Simonelli.
Cast: Renato Rascel, Silvana Pampanini, Marilyn Buferd, Luigi Pavese, Virgilio Riento, Vittorio Duse, N. Crisman, B. Corelli, M. Pisu. [No. 949]

1951
MILANA MILIARDARIA. Italian. Mambretti production. *Directors:* Vittorio Metz, Marcello Marchesi, Marino Girolami. *Script:* Metz, Marchesi. *Photography:* Tonino Delli Colli.
Cast: Toni Scotti, Isa Barzizza, D. Maggio, F. Marzi, V. Carmi, the Inter-Napoli soccer team. [No. 967]

ANNA. Italian. Archway Film Distributors. Lux Film production. *Director:* Alberto Lattuada. *Producers:* Carlo Ponti, Dino De Laurentiis. *Script:* G. Berti, Dino Risi, Ivo Perilli, F. Brusato, R. Sonego. *Photography:* Otello Martelli. *Music:* Nino Rota. *English Version:* W. de Lane Lea. *Dialogue:* Molly Stevens. 100 minutes.
Cast: Silvana Mangano, Raf Vallone, Vittorio Gassman, Jacques Dumesnil, Gaby Morlay. [No. 1000]
The De Laurentiis protégée, Silvana Mangano, was the star, Ponti's firmly in the background—and it was to be two decades more before Loren took the lead in a Lattuada film, *White Sister*.

IL MAGO PER FORZA. Italian. Amati-Mambretti production. *Directors:* Vittorio Metz, Marcello Marchesi, Marino Girolami. *Script:* Metz, Marchesi, Girolami. *Photography:* Mario Albertelli.
Cast: Toni Scotti, Dorian Gray, Mirella Umberti, Franco Volpi, Isa Barzizza, A. Rimoldi, M. Pisu, C. Lamas. [No. 1023]

IL SOGNO DI ZORRO/Zorro's Dream. Italian. I.C.S. production. *Director:* Mario Soldati. *Producer:* Niccolo Theodoli. *Script:* Vittorio Metz, Ruggero Maccari, Toni Amendola, Alessandro Continenza. *Photography:* Carlo Montuori. 93 minutes.
Cast: Walter Chiari, Delia Scala, Michele Philippe, Vittorio Gassman, Luigi Pavese, C. Ninchi, G. Tumiati, J. De Landa. [No. 1057]
Re-run of the Zorro legend, one generation on. Papa Zorro thinks his son an utter fool until a few blows to junior's numb skull turns him heroic ... Soldati went on to direct Sophia's major sex-symbol breakthrough, *Woman of the River*.

1951 continued—but Scicolone is now Lazzaro

E'ARRIVATO L'ACCORDATORE/The Tuner Has Arrived. Italian. Itala/Titanus production. *Director:* Duilio Coletti. *Script:* Mario Amendola, Ruggero Maccari, A. Borselli, Brancacci. *Photography:* Renato Del Frate. *Music:* Armando Fragna.
Cast: Nino Tarranti, Alberto Sordi, Tamara Lees, Virgilio Riento, Antonella Lualdi, Fanfulla, A. Sorrentino, C. Sposito, M. Siletta, L. Di Leo, C. Delle Piane, M. Tulli, Sofia Lazzaro. [No. 1060]
Misadventures of a hungry destitute mistaken for a piano-tuner at a rich home. Invited to dinner to avoid 13 at table, he makes sure none sit down to eat at all, while catching a band of thieves, winning £2,000 reward and the host's daughter—for whose engagement the original dinner was set ... Sofia Lazzaro's salary: 30,000 lire per day. Same again for ...

ERA LUI ... SI, SI/It's Him—Yes, Yes! Italian. Amati production. *Directors:* Vittorio Metz, Marcello Marchesi. *Producers:* Giovanni Amati, Dario Sabatello. *Script:* Metz, Marchesi, Marino Girolami. *Photography:* Tonino Delli Colli. *Music:* Nino Rota.
Cast: Walter Chiari, Silvana Pampanini, Isa Brazizza, Fanfulla, Carlo Campanini, E. Viarisio, N. Doveri, L. Rosi, L. Landi. [No. 1080]
Walter is refused a chain-store job because the boss recognises him as the nightly adversary of his dreams—when Ferdinand always loses ripe conquests to the younger man. He gets the job and

Flesh. Hungry, like Monroe, Loren stripped for *Era Lui ... Si, Si*. For the French version, the directors explained.

Era Lui ... Si, Si, 1951.

Africa sotto i mari, 1952.

the boss's dreams get worse. Walter is now stealing his wife. But it is really the daughter he is after.

1952. *Enter Sophia Loren*

LA FAVORITA. Italian. M.A.S. production. *Director:* Cesare Barlacchi. *Script:* Barlacchi—*from a play by* Rogey and Valz. *Photography:* Massimo Dallamano.
Cast: Gino Sinimberghi, Franca Tamantini, Paolo Silveri, Sophia Loren. [No. 1145]
And the registration number of this feature puts paid to the notion that the Loren name first hit cinema credits in ...

AFRICA SOTTO I MARI/Africa Under the Seas. *U.K. title:* **Woman of the Red Sea.** Italian. Gala Films distribution. Titanus-Phoenix production. *Director:* Giovanni Roccardi. *Script:* Alessandro di Stefani. *Photography:* Angelo Jannarelli. *Underwater Photography:* Giovanni Roccardi, M. Manunza. *Music:* Angelo F. Lavagnino. Ferraniacolor. 88 minutes.
Cast: Sophia Loren (*Barbara*); Steve Barclay (*Paul*); Umberto Malnati (*Sebastiano*); Antonio Bardi, Alessandro Fersen. [No. 1157]
Fictional additions to Roccardi's documentary footage brought Loren top-billing for the first time as rich, spoilt daughter of the backer of the Red Sea expedition filming fauna for TV. Paul, the yacht's skipper, is to keep a wary eye on the wilful one, and despite a hunger strike to make her centre of attention, trouble with natives, sharks and a co-starring octopus, Barbara matures from a playgirl to skipper's plaything. Film arrived in Britain in 1957, by which

time Hollywood had caught up with Loren's wet-look.

LA TRATTA DELLE BIANCHE/Girls Marked for Danger; aka. **The White Slave Trade.** Italian. Exclusive distribution. Excelsa/Ponti-De Laurentiis production. *Director:* Luigi Comencini. *Producers:* Carlo Ponti, Dino De Laurentiis. *Script:* Massimo Patrizi, Ivo Perilli. *Photography:* Antonio Trasiotti. *Editor:* Nino Baragli. *Music:* Armando Trovaioli. *Sound:* Aldo Calpini. 97 minutes. (U.K.: 67)
Cast: Eleanora Rossi Drago (*Alda*); Ettore Manni (*Carlo*); Silvana Pampanini (*Lucia*); Marc Lawrence (*Marquedi*); Vittorio Gassman (*Michele*); Enrico Salerno (*Giorgio*); Bruno Rossini (*Linuccia*); Tamara Lees (*Clara*); Sophia Loren (*Elvira*); Barbara Florian (*Fanny*). [No registration number on record]
Very much in the hackneyed tradition of the French Pigalle B-movies; white-slaver Marquedi up to nefarious tricks in a port-side town, taking revenge on Alda for missing his last shipment—by informing on her set-up boyfriend Carlo. Marquedi drums up trade by running marathon dance contests: enter Sophia on the night La Pampanini wins and is beaten to death for her troubles. The inter-gang warfare goes on with the would-be whores stuck in the middle of the affray. Film arrived in Britain five years on in tears and tatters, 30 minutes short, thereby even more disjointed than ever.

1953
AIDA.
Complete cast and details in filmography section. [No. 1241]

CAROSELLO NAPOLETANO/Neapolitan Fantasy.
Complete cast, etc., in filmography section. [No. 1297]

CI TROVIAMO IN GALLERIA/We'll Meet in the Gallery. Italian. Athene-Enic production. *Director:* Mauro Bolognini. *Script:* Fede Arnaud, Steno (Stefano Vanzina), Alessandro Continenza, Lucio Fulci, Liberati, Viganotti, Bolognini. *Photography:* Mario Scarpelli. *Music:* Carlo Rustichelli. Ferraniacolor.
Cast: Carlo Dapporto, Sophia Loren, Nilla Pizzi, Gianni Cavalieri, Alberto Sordi, Alberto Talegalli. [No. 1301]
Music-hall small-timer Gardenio is better finding than displaying talent. His sad little troupe's fortune rises when he discovers Caterina, who sings as good as she looks. They marry and he is trapped in her shadow until she secretly finances a revue for his latest stab at fame.

Ci troviamo in galleria, 1953.

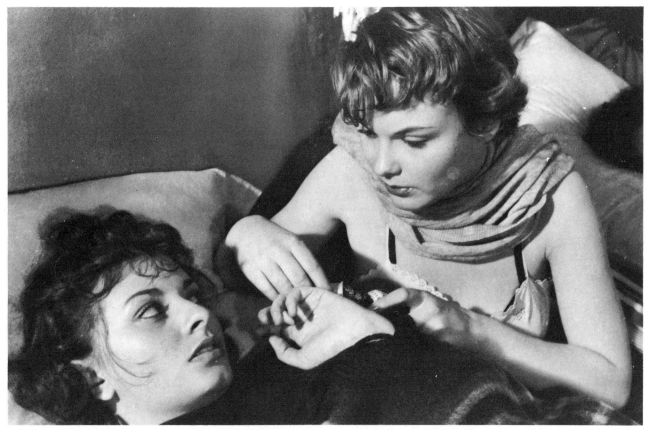

La Tratta delle bianche, 1952; her first film for Carlo Ponti.

Africa sotto i mari, 1952.

Il paese dei campanelli, 1953.

TEMPI NOSTRI/Our Times.
Complete cast, etc., in filmography section. [No. 1304]

LA DOMENICA DELLA BUONA GENTI/Good Folks' Sunday. Italian. Trionfalcine production. *Director:* Anton Guilio Majano. *Producer:* Giovanni Adessi. *Script:* Vasco Pratolini, Gian Domenico Giagni, Massimo Mida, M. Puccini, Majano. *Photography:* Alberto Albertini. *Music:* Nino Rota.
Cast: Maria Fiore, Carlo Romano, Sophia Loren, Vittorio Sanipoli, Renato Salvatori, Ave Ninchi, Alberto Talegalli, Fiorenzo Fiorentini, Marolina Boro. [No. 1315]
There are a few thousand stories in a football crowd; here were four of them. An infant daughter causes reconciliation between ex-soccer player down on his studs and wife; a pensioner's lottery flutter; a couple's on-and-off tiff; and a too newly pregnant young widow searching for her married lover with a gun in her handbag.

IL PAESE DEI CAMPANELLI. Italian. Valentina Film production. *Director:* Jean Boyer. *Producer:* Luigi De Laurentiis. *From the operetta by* Lombardo and Ranzato. Ferrianiacolor.
Cast: Sophia Loren, Carlo Dapporto, Billi and Riva, Les Frère Jacques, Achille le Togliani, Alda Mangini, Sergio Tofano, Alberto Sorrentino, Alberto Talegalli. [No. 1344]
After an opera, *Aida*—why not an operetta? Why not indeed....

UN GIORNO IN PRETURA/A Day in Court. Italian. Excelsa/Documento production. *Director:* Steno (Stefano Vanzina). *Producers:* Carlo Ponti, Dino De Laurentiis. *Script:* Lucio Fulci, Alberto

Il paese dei campanelli, 1953.

Sordi, Alessandro Continenza. *Photography:* Marco Scarpelli. 70 minutes.
Cast: Peppino De Filippo (*Judge Del Ruso*); Silvana Pampanini (*Gloriana*); Alberto Sordi (*Meniconi*); Tania Weber (*Elena*); Walter Chiari (*Don Michele*); Sophia Loren (*Anna*); Leopoldo Trieste, Virgilio Riento. [No. 1376]
Four noisy cases for the bench. Including Anna, prostitute and pick-pocket (whichever pays the better). She has lifted the wallet of a priest, Don Michele, leading to recriminations, also noisy, betwixt priest, pro and procurer.
Ten years later, post-Oscar and sandwiched between two almighty flops, *Five Miles to Midnight* and *The Condemned of Altona*, Sophia's tart little tart finally plied for trade in New York; the film has never been shown in Britain. Bosley Crowther, *New York Times*: '... all Miss Loren has to do is pretend to some slightly dramatic postures and show off her nicely tailored form ... she does it about as nicely as a bit-player might be expected to do ... but has an I'll-make-it look in her eye.'

DUE NOTTI CON CLEOPATRA/Two Nights with Cleopatra.
Complete cast, etc., in filmography section. [No. 1378]

PELLEGRINI D'AMORE/Pilgrim of Love. Italian. Pisorno production. *Director:* Andrea Forzano. *Producer:* Tullio Aleardi.
Cast: Sophia Loren, Alda Mangini, Enrico Viarisio, Charles Rutherford. [No. 1381]
Middle-aged con artists use a chorus-girl niece (Sophia) to prise easy money out of war-time enemy commanders who have both fallen for the girl in a painting hanging in their successive command H.Q. villa on the coast.

ATTILA FLAGELLO DI DIO/Attila the Hun.
Complete cast, etc., in filmography section. [No. 1392]

1954
MISERIA E NOBILTA/Poverty and Nobility. Italian. Excelsa production. *Director:* Mario Mattoli. *Script from the play by* Eduardo Scarpetta. *Photography:* Karl Strauss, Luciano Trasatti.
Cast: Toto, Sophia Loren, Enzo Turco, Franca Faldini, Dolores Palumbo, Carlo Croccoli, Valeria Moriconi. [No. 1415]
Bad blood between the poverty-sharing families of Don Felice and Don Pasquale is eased when they are asked to play the aristocratic kin of a poor ballerina hoping to marry a marquis with a stern father.

Due notti con Cleopatra, 1953, with comic Alberto Sordi (above clip). See also page 60.

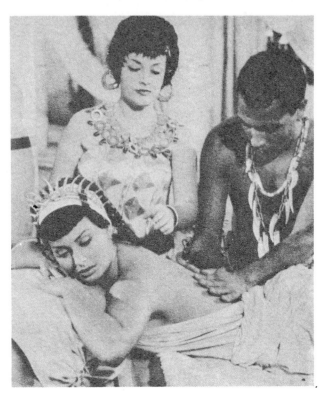

FILMOGRAPHY

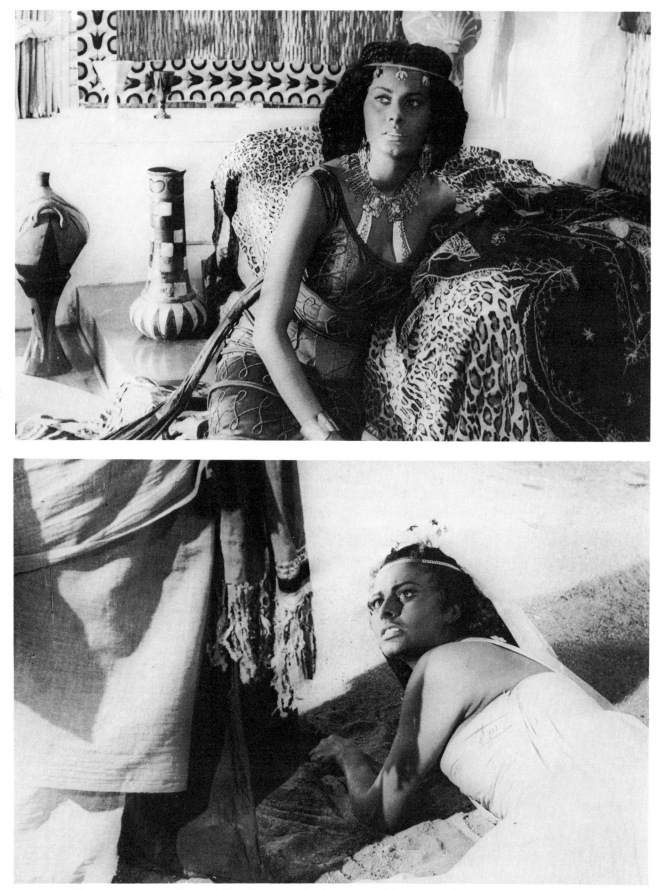

High note. Said Cecil B. DeMille: 'Around this girl you could build something really super-colossal.'

Aida

1953

Italian. Eagle Films distribution. Oscar Film production. *Director:* Clemente Fracassi. *Script:* G. Castilli, A. Gobbi, Y. Salvucci—*from the opera by* Giuseppe Verdi. *Photography:* Piero Portalupi. *Choreography:* Margherita Wallman. *Décor:* Flavio Mogherini. *Musical Supervision:* Renzo Rossellini. Ferraniacolor. 95 minutes. [No. 1241]

CAST

Sophia Loren . . . . . *Aida:* sung by Renata Tebaldi
Lois Maxwell . . . . . *Amneris:* Ebe Stignani
Luciano Della Marra *Radames:* Giuseppe Campora
Afro Poli . . . . *Amonsaro:* Gino Bechi
Antonio Cassinelli . . *Ramfis:* Giulio Neri
Enrico Formichi . . . *The Pharaoh:* Enrico Formichi

STORY

Egypt, *circa* 1230 B.C., is the setting for Verdi's cherished operatic triangle beset by war, intrigue, jealousy and a woman scorned. Amneris, daughter of the King of Egypt, loves Radames, captain of the guard. He is the victorious leader of the Egyptian army against the Ethiopians—led by King Amonsaro, father of the girl Radames secretly loves: Aida, a captured princess used by Amneris as her personal slave. Refusing to give up Aida, Radames is denounced by Amneris as a traitor and is entombed alive. Aida hides in the crypt and together they swear their eternal love as they are buried alive.

NOTES

The pin-ups were growing in popularity and number, but this was how Loren first came to the screen attention of the English-speaking world—acting the tragic Ethiopian princess and miming to the great Tebaldi, in the earliest of Afro-wigs, covered from head to toe in paint. Enough though, to make audiences stop and stare. Even DeMille took notice. Ponti noted the reaction and the die was cast.

'After drowning in my first leading role, I nearly froze to death in my second—which fell to me only because the actress the studio really wanted, Lollobrigida, considered it beneath her. The filming took place in winter in an unheated studio, and to dispel the clouds of steam coming from my mouth whenever I opened it, a make-up man kept a hair drier pointed at my lips. Years later when I visited Renata Tebaldi backstage at the Vienna Opera, she said it had been a fair exchange—my face and figure for her voice ... although she is, herself, a beautiful woman.'

Gordon Reid in *Continental Film Review*: 'Fracassi has not overcome all the obstacles inherent in his task but he gives variety to the camera without tampering with the continuity of the music ... The players, who of course mime the singing, are, for the most part, effective. Afro Poli (who is himself a singer) is first-rate and Sophia Loren and Lois Maxwell are often most expressive.'

Bosley Crowther, *New York Times*: 'Sophia Loren, the handsome girl who plays the dark-skinned and regal Aida, might just as well be singing the glorious airs that actually come from the throat of Renata Tebaldi and have been synchronised to her lip movements ... The advantage is that a fine voice is set to a stunning form and face, which is most gratifying (and unusual) in the operatic realm.'

Stand-out. Where actresses feared to tread, Loren was triumphant.

Neopolitan Fantasy

Carosello Napoletano
a.k.a. Neopolitan Carousel

1953

Italian. Archway Film Distributors. Lux production. *Director:* Ettore Giannini. *Script:* Giuseppe Marotta, Ettore Giannini, Remigio De Grosso—*from the stage presentation by* Giannini. *Photography:* Piero Portalupi. *Editor:* Nicolo Lazzari. *Costumes:* Mario Chiari. *Choreography:* Leonide Massine. *Musical Adaptation:* Raffaelo Gervasio. Eastman Color. 124 minutes. [No. 1297]

CAST

Paolo Stoppa	*Salvatore Esposito*
Clelia Matania	*His Wife*
Nadia Gray	*Naples Incarnate*
Leonide Massine	*Punchinello*
Maria Fiore	*Laundress*
Antonio	*Street Vendor*
Maria Pia Casilio	*Hairdresser*
Giacomo Rondinella	
Vittorio Caprioli	*Three Young Men*
Alberto Bonucci	
Louis Gizzi	*Mr. Gustaffson*
Sophia Loren	*Sisina*
Vera Nandi	*Lily Kansy*
Yvette Chauvire	*Donna Margherita*
Folco Lulli	*Don Raffaelo*

With the Grand Ballet de Marquis de Cueras; the Ballet Africain de Keita Fodeba; Rosita Segovia; Joan Baron's French Can-Can and singing voices of Beniamino Gigli, Carlo Tagliabue, Clelia Mantania, Giacomo Rondinella.

STORY

Grand musical evocation in Commedia dell'Arte-like mime, ballet, popular and operatic song and mass street dancing honouring the spirit of Naples from the 16th century to the (then) present day. All sketches and musical numbers were loosely linked to the adventures of Esposito, the Eternal Organ-Grinder, and his family, whose trials, tribulations and ceaseless travels remained much the same from century to century. Major set-pieces included 'The Sailor's Lament', based on a Salvatore Rosi painting of the Moorish invasion; a ballet depicting Naples Incarnate; the romance of a laundress and a hairdresser for the same street-seller; and the more tragic romance of a model for naughty postcards (Sophia Loren) and a soldier killed in the '14–18 conflict. Film closes with energetic dancing in the Napoli streets as the organ-grinder's family move on once more.

NOTES

The film brought Loren to London for her first official public appearance, being presented to the Queen and the Duke of Edinburgh when the movie opened the Italian Film Festival in 1954.

Monthly Film Bulletin: 'One regrets the excessive length, the fact that the first part is so much better than the second, the sentimental excesses of the World War I story, and the director's reliance on Massine where "Art" is concerned. Without "Art", in fact, this might have been a highly enjoyable and successful entertainment, instead of only intermittently so.'

It was 1961 and four months after the *Two Women* triumph, before the film, trimmed by 11 minutes, opened in the United States. W. H. Weiler, *New York Times*, said of Loren: 'As a somewhat lachrymose soubrette of the music-halls at the turn of the century, she is as physically imposing as ever, if not as spirited.'

One credit missing from above, possibly a first in screen history, is that accorded to Serafino Coccio and Sons. They supplied the fireworks. From here on, Sophia Loren looked after that department herself....

Our Times

Tempi Nostri, a.k.a. Anatomy of Love [U.S.]

1953

Italo-French. Lux/Cines (Rome)/Lux du France (Paris) co-production. *Director:* Alessandro Blasetti. *Script Continuity:* Suso Cecchi d'Amico, Blasetti—*from stories by* Vasco Paratolini, Alberto Moravia, Giuseppe Marotta, Marioni Morelli, Silvio d'Arzo, Ercole Palti, Achille Campanilli, Alessandro Continenza, Basilio Franchina, Ennio Flaino, Luigi Filippo d'Amicco, Chiarini, Biancoli, Marinucci, Carancinci, De Caro, Bassani. *Photography:* Gabor Pogany. *Music:* Alessandro Cicognini. 92 minutes. [No. 1304]

CAST

Vittorio De Sica, Sophia Loren, Toto, Lea Padovani, Marcello Mastroianni, Alba Arnova, Elisa Cegani, Eduardo de Filippo, Danielle Delorme, Yves Montand, Francois Perrier, Dany Robin, Michel Simon, Sylvie.

STORY

Mixed bag of sketches contrasting Blasetti's *Altri Tempi* with the current Italian situation. Ranging from De Sica and Elisa Cegani as threadbare aristos re-living past glories as film extras to Michel Simon saving Sylvie's suicide bid. From Moravia's poignant sob-story of Mastroianni and Padovani trying to abandon their starving baby to De Sica, again, as a lustful Neapolitan busman. Plus Sophia modelling almost silently for a bug-eyed Toto and his new camera: *La Macchina Fotografica.*

NOTES

Altri Tempi/Times Gone By dealt with yesterday; *Tempi Nostri* was today ... with a lot of hints about tomorrow. The first film's line-up had included De Sica with Lollobrigida; the second was the start of the De Sica, Mastroianni, Loren teaming, if in separate embryo for now. Also among the hefty writing team were six of Loren's future scenarists. However, the film never reached Britain and did not arrive in America until the same month as *That Kind of Woman.* The difference in the two kinds of Loren must have been startling.

Bosley Crowther, *New York Times*, found it disappointing after *Altri Tempi.* 'As for Toto's interest in Sophia Loren in the fifth [story], it is that of a burlesque comedian for a girl with a noticeable shape. As a fellow who buys a camera so he may have the fun of photographing her, he runs through a standard routine of wiggling his nostrils and popping his eyes. The age of this picture is maybe gathered from the fact that Miss Loren's role is merely that of a shapely stooge for the clown.'

Stooge. Playing the pin-up for farceur Toto; it was, at that time, the story of her life.

Two Nights With Cleopatra

Due Notti con Cleopatra

1953

Italian. An Excelsa-Rosa production. *Director:* Mario Mattoli. *Script:* Ruggero Maccari. *Photography:* Karl Strauss, Riccardo Pallottini. Ferrianiacolor. [No. 1378]

CAST

Sophia Loren . . . . *Cleopatra/Nisca*
Alberto Sordi . . . . *Cesarino*
Ettore Manni, Paul Muller, Alberto Talegalli.

STORY

Egypt, 31 B.C. Affairs of state keep Cleopatra at her palace and far from Mark Anthony before the battle with Octavius. She finds enough time, though, to spend each night with some unfortunate member of her guard. Unfortunate, because come the morning, the lover is swiftly executed. Newly commissioned Cesarino cannot understand the lack of enthusiasm for guard duty and welcomes such royal patronage when his time arrives. His colleagues are stunned to find him alive and well next morning. It was not Cleopatra he dallied and played with, but a double the queen had found to take her place to enable her, finally, to slip away to Anthony's embrace. On the second night it is the real Cleopatra in the bedchamber—and only the quick wit of the adoring double, Nisca, saves the young guard officer from his prescribed fate.

NOTES

Carry on Cleo—Italian Style. Sadly the film—really a case of Two Nights with Two Cleopatras—never came to Britain in any shape or form.

On February 24, 1959, according to his diary, Hollywood producer Walter Wanger discussed the possibility of Sophia Loren playing the queen again—as the lady in his ultimately headline-making *Cleopatra* project. Carlo Ponti said Sophia would be interested. 20th Century-Fox also considered Bardot, Monroe, Novak, Hayward, Lollobrigida, Jennifer Jones and Audrey Hepburn. Wanger stuck with his original fancy: Liz Taylor. He was wrong. Loren would have been perfect in the rôle. And for half the money, no trouble at all and twice the profit.

Dual rôle. Sophia played Cleopatra and her equally statuesque blonde slave (below; with co-star Alberto Sordi).

Attila The Hun

Attila flagello di Dio, a.k.a. Attila

1953

Italo-French. Archway Film Distributors. Lux (Rome)/Ponti-De Laurentiis/Lux (Paris) co-production. *Director:* Pietro Francisci. *Producer:* Giorgio Adriani. *Script:* Ennio De Concini, Primo Zeglo, Ivo Perilli, Frank Gervasi. *Photography:* Aldo Tonti, Karl Strauss. *Editor:* Leo Catozzo. *Music:* Enzio Masetti. *Art Director:* Flavio Mogherini. *Sound:* Aldo Capini, Biagio Fiorelli. Technicolor. 79 minutes. [No. 1392]

CAST

Anthony Quinn	*Attila*
Sophia Loren	*Honoria*
Henri Vidal	*Ezio*
Irene Papas	*Grune*
Ettore Manni	*Bleda*
Claude Laydu	*Valentinian*
Colette Regis	*Galla Placidia*
Eduardo Cianelli	*Onegesius*

STORY

Roman general Ezio fails in winning peace terms with Attila, leader of the barbaric Huns threatening the corrupt Ravenna court of Emperor Valentinian. Ezio is imprisoned for treason yet refuses the enticing offer of the emperor's scheming sister, Honoria, to marry her and depose Valentinian. She next offers herself to Attila himself—plus half her kingdom. He orders her slain and drives his hordes on to bloody pillage, destroying all in their path across the Alps to Italy. Ezio is placed back at the head of the army, but once killed in battle it is left to Pope Leo the Great to stop Attila at the gates of Rome. A miraculous storm violently erupts as Attila orders his final advance; his terrified Huns fall back in disorder to the North. Faith is victorious; Rome is safe; Attila departs leaving his mark and name as a symbol for all future savage warfare.

NOTES

End of Loren's busiest year in movies—ten films inside 12 months, and the penultimate production in the first massive Ponti-De Laurentiis push for international prominence which began with Kirk Douglas, Quinn again and Dino's La Mangano in *Ulysses*. That worked; this didn't. Not with Quinn's Attila bellowing, with the help of four writers: 'Today Rome—tomorrow the world'!

The British Film Institute's *Monthly Film Bulletin* thought the production lavish and closely modelled on the Hollywood spectacular, particularly in its sanctimonious climax; Richard W. Nason, *New York Times*, insisted: 'Hollywood in its most delinquent mood could not improve on the pointless degree of violence and piety that the Italian film-makers have poured together in *Attila*.'

Loren looked fine; Quinn bored. He was much more into the small-budget affair he was making at the same time to end his five-picture contract—Fellini's *La Strada*. This became the first official (non-honorary) foreign movie Oscar-winner in 1956. Ponti and De Laurentiis had arrived. Sophia could not be far behind. She was not: five more years....

Output. The end of Loren's busiest movie year—she made ten movies within the twelvemonth ... and her name.

Gold Of Naples

L'Oro di Napoli, a.k.a. Every Day's a Holiday [U.S.]

1954

Italian. Gala Film Distributors. Ponti-De Laurentiis production. *Director:* Vittorio De Sica. *Producers:* Dino De Laurentiis, Carlo Ponti. *Script:* Cesare Zavattini, Vittorio De Sica, Giuseppe Marotta—*from* Marotta's *novel. Photography:* Otello Martelli. *Editor:* Evaldo da Roma. *Music:* Alessandro Cicognini. 135 minutes. 107 in U.K., 74 in U.S. [No. 1423]

CAST
Pizzas on Credit or *The Ring*

Sophia Loren . . . . *Sofia*
Giacomo Furia . . . . *Husband*
Paolo Stoppa . . . . *Widower*
Alberto Farnes . . . . *Sofia's Lover*

The other three episodes, entitled *The Racketeer*, *The Gambler* and *Theresa*, featured Toto, Vittorio De Sica and Silvana Mangano.

STORY (*Pizzas on Credit* or *The Ring*)
Pizza-seller Sofia loses her wedding ring during another tryst with her lover. Seeing her husband's mounting consternation, she assures him it must have dropped into the morning's dough—which means a fast, furious foray among the day's customers. While the hunt goes on, the boyfriend returns the ring and saves Sofia's reputation—though not her husband's suspicions.

NOTES
A gusty, busty Neapolitan, full of life, vigour and figure—and called Sofia. The rôle seemed a natural for the vibrant new girl on the Rome scene. De Sica, having already unleashed the best of Lollobrigida on to the world, was well pleased with Loren after a meeting in Ponti's office. Co-producer Dino De Laurentiis, however, wanted a bigger name. Lollo even? De Sica stuck firm. 'We've got to take Loren. We've nobody else who fits. Besides, she won't want much money.' 'Take her then,' said Dino. 'But you'll regret it.'

Dino was wrong, De Sica was right, Sophia was a bag of nerves, 'my throat was dry, my legs stiff, somehow I managed it', and *Time* magazine rejoiced. '[Her] self-congratulating look seemed to say, look at me, I'm all woman and it will be a long time before you see such a woman again. She took a long, unforgettable walk in the rain through the streets of the city, drinking the applause of venal eyes.' (And as it happened, catching bronchial pneumonia from the artificial downpours.)

Less in awe was the *Monthly Film Bulletin*, presumably because of the manner in which the film had been sliced about. Originally, there had been six episodes. The complete version was seen in Britain at the 1955 Edinburgh Festival only. Missing from this Gala release was the sketch featuring Eduardo De Filippo and the compassionate reportage of a child's funeral procession; better though than an English-dubbed treatment for the United States, re-titled, *Every Day's a Holiday*, which cut De Sica's yarn completely and excised Paolo Stoppa from the Loren tale. Mercifully, this version was trade-shown once in London and never opened. 'De Sica,' said the *M.F.B.*, 'while retaining the trappings of neo-realism, has turned, none too happily, to the conventions of the more commercial type of Italian film ...' With Loren firmly in tow, he was to continue along this path, and though the *Monthly Film Bulletin* rarely agreed, the results were often vastly entertaining.

Tryst. Pizza-seller Sophia and lover Alberto Farnes.

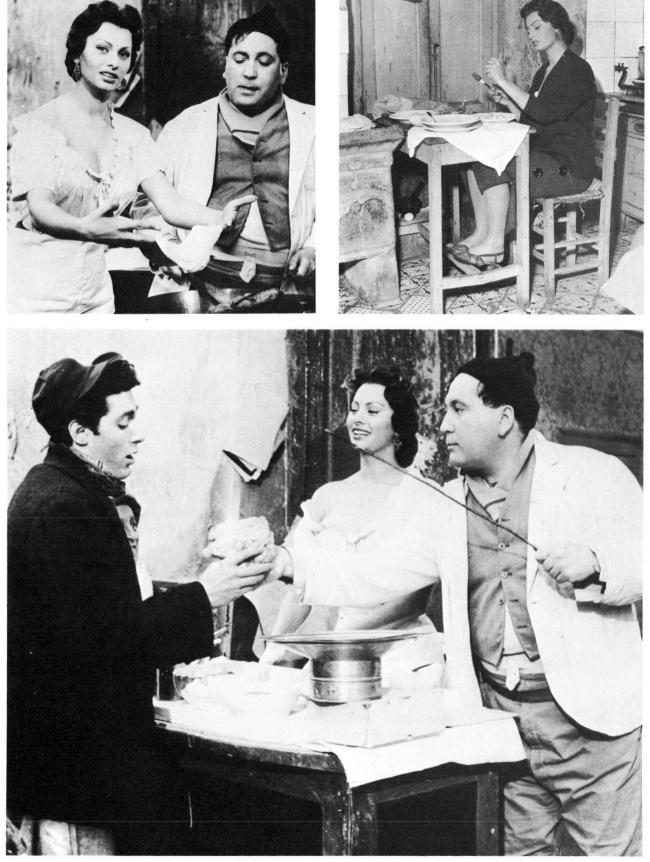

Trust. Ponti knew the rôle was right for her and De Sica was rapidly persuaded.
Their belief was rewarded—with a new star.

Woman Of The River

La Donna del Fiume

1954

Franco-Italian. Columbia Pictures release. Excelsa Films/Les Films de Centaur co-production. *Director:* Mario Soldati. *Producer:* Basilio Franchina. *Script:* Basilio Franchina, Giorgio Bassani, Pier Paolo Pasolini, Florestano Vancini, Antonio Altoviti, Mario Soldati—*from an idea by* Ennio Flaiano, Alberto Moravia. *Dialogue:* Giorgio Bassani, Pier Paolo Pasolini. *Photography:* Otello Martelli. *Editor:* Leo Cattozzo. *Art Director:* Flavio Mogherini. *Décor:* Arrigo Breschi. *Music:* Angelo F. Lavagnino, Armando Trovaioli. *Choreography:* Leo Coleman. *Sound:* Paolo Uccello, Bruno Monreal, Aldo Calpini. Technicolor. 95 minutes. [No. 1499]

CAST

Sophia Loren . . . . *Nives Mongolini*
Gerard Oury . . . . *Enzo Cinti*
Lise Bourdin . . . . *Tosca*
Rik Battaglia . . . . *Gino Lodi*
Enrico Olivierei . . . . *Oscar*

STORY

Peasant beauty Nives, sultriest girl at the eel-canning factory, refuses police officer Cinti's pro-

Mamina. All-woman—and her first maternal rôle.

posal; she prefers trawlerman Gino and eagerly gives herself to him. He moves to another town immediately and a pregnant Nives follows to warn him that the police suspect his nightly smuggling activities. Gino insults her, presuming she is blackmailing him to the altar. Heartbroken, she informs Cinti about Gino's smuggling and he is jailed. Two years later, Cinti traces Nives to the mouth of the river Po, where she cuts cane to support her son, and warns her that Gino has escaped from prison. Instead of revenge, the runaway's feeling is of despair only when he arrives to learn his son has been drowned in the river. Gino surrenders as he watches Nives at their son's funeral procession in the village.

NOTES

Six scriptwriters! Including the director, the producer and the novice Pier Paolo Pasolini. When not a word was required, Loren's body told all. Ponti obviously decided on the best only for his star, even though the premise was so simple. Repeat his partner De Laurentiis' breakthrough formula for his wife Silvana Mangano and re-visit 1949's *Bitter Rice/Riso Amora*. La Loren proved better, hotter, more stimulating and erotic even when stood around in her '55 hot-pants and gum-boots. (Ponti was to repeat the idea yet again in '61 with the thinner-than-slim Elsa Martinelli among the *Rice Girls*. The age of the mini-skirt has since stilled Po-power. Or has it?)
Columbia Pictures grabbed the film and sold it fast and hugely—'A Story of a Girl Who Wanted Love for a Lifetime!' 'Desired by the Lawkeeper and the Lawbreaker!'—and it proved the first general British release for 'the sensational Italian actress whose beauty has made her one of the world's most popular cover girls' as the posters screamed. Caught up in the excitement, London's critics went potty about the Po girl.
Picturegoer: 'Everyone who's ever seen a pin-up of Sophia Loren knows she's all female and then some. But what an actress, too! That's the surprising thing. And the combination of such an actress and such a woman is pretty terrific.'
Felix Barker, *Evening News:* 'It is a typical Italian dish in which the ingredients are sex, pictorial beauty

Lift-off. 'Carlo never told me he was risking everything on me.' Six writers and Rik Battaglia as screen-lover.

and tragedy, served very hot ... Plunged into such a cataclysm, Sophia Loren does not have a moment to prove if she has any subtlety as an actress. Too quickly she is rushed from the proud beauty who spurns the hero to the passion-drenched mistress and on to the red-eyed, weeping and bereft mother. She is all that those pin-ups have led us to hope, but I do not think she can be conceded many points over the incomparable Lollo (who certainly has far more sense of humour) until we have seen her again ...'
Milton Shulman, *Evening Standard*: 'But this heavy-breathing plot is merely an excuse for the display of the sultry talents of Miss Sophia Loren. She is a graduate of the Italian school of acting which some-one has described as having only two expressions—horizontal and vertical. The camera clings relentlessly to her, surveying her up and down like some short-sighted archaeologist studying a Roman wall. Whether she is jiving with ecstasy or weeping with remorse, the camera angle is always titivating ...'
Peter Burnup, *News of the World*: 'Sultry, seductive and altogether lovely ... the matchless Loren. To me she's lovelier and more fascinating than even La Lollo and Anna Magnani ...'
Ponti could not have written that better himself.

Too Bad She's Bad

Peccato che sia una Canaglia

1954

Italian. Gala Films. Documento Film production. *Director:* Alessandro Blasetti. *Script:* Alessandro Continenza, Suso Cecchi d'Amico, Ennio Flaiano— *from a story by* Alberto Moravia. *Photography:* Aldo Giordani. *Editor:* Mario Serandrei. *Art Director:* Mario Chiari. *Sound:* Ennio Sensi. 96 minutes. [No. 1519]

CAST

Sophia Loren	*Lina*
Vittorio De Sica	*Sopriano*
Marcello Mastroianni	*Paolo*
Umberto Malmatti	*Stolen Wallet*
Margherita Bagni	*His Wife*
Mario Scaccia	*Stolen Bag*
Wanda Benedetti	*His Wife*
Mario Passante	*Commissioner*
Memo Carotenuto	*Cesare*
Giacomo Furi	*Luigi*
Lina Furi	*His Wife*

STORY

Driving the lovely Lina and three young men to the beach, taxi-driver Paolo decides to join their swimming antics, when he finds they are really trying to steal his cab. He attempts to take Lina to the police, but her involved explanations confuse him thoroughly and on meeting her gentle father, Sopriano, he decides they must, basically, be an honest family. Until he ... discovers that the gold cigarette case Lina gave him is stolen ... finds Sopriano lifting a suitcase at the rail station ... and later on, being helped by Lina to pick pockets on a bus. The family is crooked, every last shapely one of them. Paolo hustles the entire brood to the *carabinieri*, but his accusations become empty gesticulations as the quick-witted, fast-talking father and daughter team of con-artists talk themselves out of trouble without batting an eye. In desperation, Paolo proposes to Lina to keep her straight. She accepts, joyfully: he is the first prize she has not had to steal.

NOTES

Towards the end of the Po river locations for her previous film, Sophia Loren was relaxing on the river bank when she noticed a solitary rowing boat

Idea. Blasetti used inspired casting ...

Trio. Blasetti matched Loren with De Sica and Mastroianni and gave birth to Italy's most memorable screen team.

headed straight for her. A man got out, a handkerchief protecting his head from the sun. 'I want you for my next film,' he gasped. She did not, at first, recognise Blasetti—who had last used her as little more than a stooge in *Tempi Nostri*. Other sketches in that movie had featured De Sica and Mastroianni. This time Blasetti put the trio together: and his film is the genesis of the most successful partnership in Italian movies. They worked superbly from the start, despite, as far as the British release version was concerned, a patently farcical attack of ultra-English dubbing. *Picturegoer* moaned that she sounded like a Roman from Roedean. 'The shrugs, the sighs, the wiggle, however, are very definitely Continental.'

Bosley Crowther, *New York Times*: 'One striking point in its favour is the luxurious Sophia Loren, who is something to look at from any angle or any

side ... she displays such a full and shapely figure she makes it a pleasure to consider being robbed. And don't think the lady doesn't know it. With her, ambulating is an art. Leaning over is an aesthetic manœuvre. The *signorina* racks up quite a score.'

Gordon Reid, *Continental Film Review*: 'Sophia plays the wayward daughter of an elderly thief of gallant charm (De Sica) and she seems to have acquired something of this actor's assurance and attack.'

Monthly Film Bulletin: 'Turning to the acting in the film raises some fundamental problems concerning the craft of dubbing. Sophia Loren's brand of jolly, uninhibited sex-appeal is not enhanced by the substitution of a precise English voice of considerable gentility.'

Carlo Ponti, meantime, was drafting a cable: 'Learn English. You're going to need it soon.'

The Sign Of Venus

Il Segno di Venere

1955

Femme fatale. To Raf Vallone's fireman ...

... Alberto Sordi's inept car thief ...

Italian. Gala Films. Titanus production. *Director:* Dino Risi. *Producer:* Marcello Girosi. *Script:* Luigi Comencini, Franca Valeri, Agenore Incrocci, Ennio Flaiano, Cesare Zavattini—*from a story by* Chekhov. *Photography:* Carlo Montuori. *Editor:* Mario Serandrei. *Music:* Renzo Rossellini. *Art Director:* Gaston Medin. *Sound:* Kurt Doubrawsky. 98 minutes. [No. 1560]

CAST

Franca Valeri . . . . *Cesira*
Sophia Loren . . . . *Agnese*
Raf Vallone . . . . *Ignazio*
Vittorio De Sica . . . . *Alessio Spano*
Alberto Sordi . . . . *Romolo Proietti*
Peppino de Filippo . . . . *Mario*
Virgilio Riento . . . . *Agnese's Father*
Tina Pica . . . . *Agnese's Aunt*

STORY

Cesira and Agnese are cousins, complete opposites in dreams and gleams, living with Agnese's father and old aunt in a small Rome flat. Agnese is an unconscious *femme fatale*, attracting men like flies and wishing she did not. Cesira, from Milan, less attractive, more provincial, does not attract anything close to romance and wishes she did, and is much elated when a fortune-teller explains that she is under the sign of Venus and much favoured by the goddess of love. Her circle does not offer much hope, however; Mario is a middle-aged photographer; Romolo, a petty thief of cars; and Alessio Spano, a grasping writer. They all take advantage of her good nature to further their own pockets and schemes. Not even Ignazio, the virile fireman, is attracted to her as she hoped—but to Agnese whom he makes pregnant. Cesira runs away, all illusions shattered: Romolo is arrested and Alessio, in the unkindest cut of all, goes off with the fortune-teller.

NOTES

A well-timed break from centre-stage for Loren as she plays second fiddle to Franca Valeri (who also helped write the screenplay), and collects an important acting lesson in an effective, against-the-image part. Enough so for *Films and Filming* to

... and Vittorio De Sica's cutting portrait of a seedy poet of sorts. Loren learned from them all.

comment drily: 'Sophia Loren supplements the promise established by her *Woman of the River*. She may well do great things if she does not see too many Susan Hayward films in the meantime.'

Campbell Dixon, *Daily Telegraph*: '... the mood, the gentle pathos, the slightly astringent humour may all be traced back to the master [Chekhov], but so freshly are the ingredients mixed that something I liked at a foreign festival seems even more enjoyable on a second viewing ... De Sica plays the shabby, flamboyant poet with superb panache; and he would be a queer sort of fellow who didn't accept Miss Loren's charms, like certain truths, as self-evident, if not inalienable.'

The Miller's Wife

La Bella Mugnaia

1955

Italian. Gala Films. Titanus/Ponti-De Laurentiis production. *Director:* Mario Camerini. *Producers:* Carlo Ponti, Dino De Laurentiis. *Script:* Mario Camerini, Ennio De Concini, Alessandro Continenza, Ivo Perilli—*from the play by* Pedro de Alarcon. *Photography:* Enzo Serafin. *Music:* A. F. Lavagnino. *Art Director:* Guido Fiorini. *Sound:* Mario Morigi. CinemaScope. Eastmancolor. 91 minutes. [No. 1598]

CAST

Sophia Loren . . . . *Carmela*
Vittorio De Sica . . . . *The Governor*
Marcello Mastroianni . . . . *Luca, the Miller*
Paolo Stoppa . . . . *Gardunia*
Yvonne Sanson . . . . *Governor's Wife*
Carletto Sposito and Virgilio Riento.

STORY

Naples 1680 is ruled by a randy Spanish governor. Not content with oppressing peasants with extortionate taxes, he busily covets their wives: Luca, the miller's, in particular. To remove Luca and make his conquest of Carmela easier, the Governor has him jailed on trumped-up sedition charges and makes straight for the mill waving a free pardon in the air. Carmela can have it—at the right price. Carmela is no fool. Drugging the governor's drink, she snatches the pardon and fleet-foots it to the prison. Luca, meantime, has escaped, returned home, misread all the evidence, assumed his wife has succumbed ... and decides to take the Governor's wife in rapid revenge. He stops short, just, of actual rape when she suggests another way for the peasants to teach the roving-eyed Governor a lesson ...

NOTES

It's that trio again—becoming more deft a comedy team with every scene. Helped by a director who knew his story well—he had filmed it before as *The Three Cornered Hat* in 1934. Camerini knew De Sica even better, having directed the actor's screen début

Men Are Such Rascals in 1932.

Bosley Crowther, *New York Times*: 'Miss Loren is a monument to her sex and the mere opportunity to observe her is a privilege not to be missed.'

Gordon Reid, *Continental Film Review*: 'The bright, yellow sun of the Naples area, the colour, the superb beauty of Sophia Loren, the comedy playing of De Sica, the friendly charm of Mastroianni, combine in a light entertainment on a theme that has become, perhaps, too familiar via story (Alarcon), ballet (Falla), opera (Wolf). But Sophia has never looked more devastating.'

But then, like many of her Hollywood rivals, she found she was made for CinemaScope.

Scandal In Sorrento

Pane, Amore e . . .

1955

Italo-French. Gala Films. Titanus, Rome/S.G.C. (Paris) co-production. *Director:* Dino Risi. *Producer:* Marcello Girosi. *Script:* Ettore Margadonna, Marcello Girosi, Vincenzo Talarico, Dino Risi. *Photography:* Giuseppe Rotunno. *Editor:* Mario Serandrei. *Art Director:* Gastone Medin. *Sound:* Kurt Doubrawsky. CinemaScope. Eastmancolor. 85 minutes. [No. 1623]

CAST

Sophia Loren . . . . *Donna Sofia*
Vittorio De Sica . . . . . . *Marasciallo Carotenuto*
Lea Padovani . . . . *Donna Violante*
Antonio Cifariello . . . . . *Nicolino*
Mario Carotenuto . . . . . . *Don Matteo*
Joka Berretty . . . . *Erika*
Tina Pica . . . . *Housekeeper*

STORY

The ever-amorous police chief Carotenuto returns home to Sorrento, accompanied by his faithful old housekeeper. He has command of the *carabinieri* of his birthplace, but his cup is not quite running over. He cannot live in his own house. Sofia, the local fish-seller—known as The Heckler—has been renting his home in his absence and refuses to quit. And Carmella, the housekeeper, agrees with her— typically. He puts up at an attractive spinster's house—and puts up with the dancing overtures of Sofia, using her distinct charms to persuade him to help her lover, Nicolino, pass his police exams. Infatuated with the girl, the Marshal is determined to

Mutual Admiration Society. Sophia joins up
with De Sica again . . .

marry her, defying all warnings of his brother, Don Matteo, the town's priest. Annoyed by Nicolino's jealousy, Sofia agrees to wed. But once Carotenuto realises she still loves the lad, he arranges their reconciliation—and begins to take a second look at his landlady, Donna Violante.

NOTES

Another Loren inheritance from Gina Lollobrigida—the biggest to date and the last, discounting *Lady L* ten years later. The previous two films in the *Pane, Amore e ...*/*Bread, Love and ...* series, in which the stylish De Sica chased La Lollo up and down an Abruzzi hillside township, had been major hits throughout Europe. Then came the blown-up rivalry between the mammarian goddesses. Lollo quit the series and it was inevitable that Loren should replace her. She had De Sica on her side still—plus CinemaScope and colour which Lollo never had. Did the switch work? The Italians did not seem to mind, but British critics were, as always, in two minds.

Reg Whitley, *Daily Mirror*: 'What an impact Sophia makes, even in the simple garb of a girl behind a fish counter. What pep she puts into her love scenes! And what a mambo she dances with him before the old boy realises he has been taken for a ride. Sophia shows once more that she is one of the few stars who combine sex appeal with acting skill. She is terrific in this lighthearted, colourfully set picture, which is Italy's current smash hit.'

Monthly Film Bulletin: 'Sophia Loren, who proves a poor substitute for Gina Lollobrigida, exudes little real charm and, contrary to expectations, the beautiful settings of the Bay of Naples are only tentatively explored.'

Peter John Dyer, *Films and Filming*: 'De Sica's accomplished charm and Loren's determined verve pull us through some tepid situations'.

A. H. Weiler, *New York Times*: 'Much of the film's footage is vivid illustration that Signorina Loren in a tight bodice or writhing through a mambo dance in a low-cut flaming red gown is likely to raise the temperature of any red-blooded citizen.'

De Sica killed off the series in his own production of *Pane, Amore e Andalusia* opposite Carmen Sevilla in Spain in 1958.

... and young Antonio Cifariello in another project dropped by La Lollo.

Lucky To Be A Woman

La Fortuna di Essere Donna

1955

Italo-French. Intercontinental Film Distributors. Le Louvre Films (Paris)/Documento Films (Rome) co-production. *Director:* Alessandro Blasetti. *Producer:* Raymond Alexandre. *Script:* Susso Cecchi d'Amico, Ennio Flaiano, Alessandro Continenza, Alessandro Blasetti. *Photography:* Otello Martelli. *Editor:* Mario Serandrei. *Music:* Alessandro Cicognini. *Art Director:* Franco Lolli. *Sound:* Ennio Sensi. Panoramic screen. 91 minutes. [No. 1655]

Mastroianni discovers her.

Boyer French-polishes her.

CAST

Sophia Loren	*Antoinette*
Charles Boyer	*Count Gregorio*
Marcello Mastroianni	*Corrado*
Nino Besozzi	*Film Producer*
Titina de Filippo	*Antoinette's Mother*
Giustino Duran	*Antoinette's Father*

Elisa Gegani, Mauro Sacripante, Memmo Carotenuto.

STORY

Stunning Rome girl, Antoinette, is suddenly sprung on the road to fame and fortune—stardom!—via a candid newspaper shot of her adjusting her stockings. Corrado took the shots and smooths her future by introducing her to suave impresario Count Gregorio. Much taken with her potential, the count teaches her how to behave like a lady—with striking success. There is much talk of a Gregorio contract, if they marry. Corrado, meantime, is left secretly pining for the girl in his lens. And it is while strolling home together after a party one night, that Antoinette realises her love for the photographer outweighs anything offered by a ritzy career.

NOTES

Apart from Charles Boyer in the obvious De Sica rôle, it is the spring-autumn triangle as before, lacking not only De Sica's presence, but his effect on both Loren and Mastroianni.

Monthly Film Bulletin: 'The star, Sophia Loren, is surrounded by numerous male satellites variously concerned to seduce her or to advance their own financial interests through her, while she sways unconcernedly through the commotion. But not even she, or the characteristic performances of Charles Boyer and Marcello Mastroianni, relieve the tedium of this commonplace film.'

Then again, it could be fatigue. It was Loren's 17th film in three years! A hectic semester—leading to glowing graduation, Hollywood style.

Come wiz me? For a change De Sica's suave philanderer was played by Charles Boyer.

Boyer admired her greatly ...

... but Marcello, of course, won her.

The Pride And The Passion

1957

Exportise. Enter Hollywood's bravura.

American. United Artists. Stanley Kramer Films production. *Director/Producer:* Stanley Kramer. *Script:* Edna and Edward Anhalt—*from the novel* The Gun *by* C. S. Forester. *Photography:* Franz Planer. *Editors:* Frederick Knudson, Ellsworth Hoagland. *Music:* George Antheil. *Art Director:* Fernando Carrera. *Choreography:* Paco Reyes. *Sound:* Walter Elliott, Bates Mason. *Military Adviser:* Lieut.-Col. Luis Cano. *Main Titles:* Saul Bass. VistaVision. Technicolor. 130 minutes.

CAST

Cary Grant . . . . *Capt. Anthony Trumbull*
Frank Sinatra . . . . *Miguel*
Sophia Loren . . . . *Juana*
Theodore Bikel . . . . . . *Gen. Jouvet*
John Wengraf . . . . *Sermaine*
Jay Novello . . . . *Ballinger*
Jose Nieto . . . . *Carlos*
Carlos Larranaga . . . . . *Jose*
Philip van Zandt . . . . . *Vidal*
Paco el Laberinto . . . . . *Manolo*

STORY

Spain 1810. Capt. Anthony Trumbull, R.N., is ordered to locate and commandeer a huge cannon abandoned by the Spanish army in their retreat from Napoleon's invasion. Guerrillas alone carry on any persistent struggle against occupation and Trumbull contacts *guerrillero* leader Miguel; together they raise the cannon from a deep ravine and make all necessary repairs to the awesome weapon. Miguel refuses to hand it over to Trumbull, however, insisting it must first be used by his band in an attack on the French garrison at Avila. This necessitates a journey of marathon proportions across the Spanish map—in daily danger from French troops and local informers. During the epic trek, Trumbull falls in love with Juana, a pretty camp follower originally attached to Miguel. Finally, Miguel readies his massed peasants, Trumbull trains the great gun on the Avila walls and after fierce, bloody fighting —cannon-shot and hand-to-hand—the *guerrilleros*

Finesse. Experts, yes, by the dozen; Cary Grant alone though recognised her true potential.

succeed in storming the city. Searching the battle-field, Trumbull finds the dead bodies of both Miguel and Juana, and he carries them into the city they had freed.

NOTES
The re-birth of the epic. Taking a leaf or three out of DeMille's book, with the modern-day approach of shooting it where it happened, Stanley Kramer spent six million dollars (200,000 of them on Loren, the ex-extra of *Quo Vadis*) and quite a few more on Sinatra, despite their lack of *simpatico* on *Not as a Stranger*, in the rôle Brando refused, plus months galore of gore and bore in Spain shooting the Forester book. Much of it did not entirely come off. For once in an epic, the crowd scenes—the shifting, surging forces moving that damnable cannon—were impressive; the stellar leads were not.

While Loren was well suited to her rôle, she experienced the first painful difficulties of acting in English, and working with an American director. Her co-stars, both totally mis-cast, were soon conquered by the Loren charm, however. Sinatra, who was, to say the least, less than happy with being stuck in one country (let alone one place) for four months, was moved enough to deliver the immortal phrase: She is a gasser. Grant said more, much more. And Sophia returned the compliment, mixing

Tradition. Loren dancing had become a must.

79

The Voice. When Frank Sinatra met The Shape he called her 'a gasser'. What else?

in with Sinatra's Hollywood slanguage and having everyone falling in love with her—even the critics, who wisely left her alone and concentrated on the wider vistas. Said Jympson Harman, *Evening News*: 'the excitement is tremendous ... undoubtedly one of the most amazing spectacles of all time.'

Charles Swann, *Picturegoer*: 'A very, very quiet explosion. The near negligent provocation of her Italian films—and even *Boy on a Dolphin*—is gone ... Two scenes ... show what Loren, in unrestraint, can do. One is when she flaunts herself at Cary Grant. Says she: "I think you'd like to behave more like a man than a piece of cold mutton." After that invitation any piece of cold mutton would want to sit up and beg. The other? When she dances the flamenco to the throbbing of guitars and the rhythmic handclaps of the peasants. You see that Loren has escaped from the trite character so apparent in the other dull scenes.'

Bosley Crowther, *New York Times*: '... And Sophia Loren as the lovely camp follower, who shifts her affection from the first to the second man, has mostly to play a sweet peacemaker and string along with the gang.'

And New Yorkers strung along with her. This was her fourth film to arrive in the one year (1957), with *The Miller's Wife*, *Scandal in Sorrento* and *The Pride* all opening within a fortnight.

Ex-extra. Seven years after being in the crowd herself.

Boy On A Dolphin

1957

American. 20th Century-Fox. *Director:* Jean Negulesco. *Producer:* Samuel G. Engel. *Script:* Ivan Moffat, Dwight Taylor—*from the novel by* David Divine. *Photography:* Milton Krasner. *Photo-effects:* Ray Kellog. *Editor:* William Mace. *Music:* Hugo Friedhofer. *Conductor:* Lionel Newman. *Art Directors:* Lyle R. Wheeler, Jack Martin Smith. *Sound:* W. D. Flock, H. M. Leonard. *Song:* Boy on a Dolphin, *based on* Tin Afto *by* Takis Morakis; *American Lyrics:* Paul Francis Webster. CinemaScope. Eastmancolor. 111 minutes.

CAST

Alan Ladd	*James Calder*
Clifton Webb	*Victor Parmalee*
Sophia Loren	*Phaedra*
Alexis Minotis	*Government Man*
Jorge Mistral	*Rhif*
Laurence Naismith	*Dr. Hawkins*
Piero Giagnoni	*Niko*
Gertrude Flynn	*Miss Dill*
Charles Fawcett	
Charlotte Terrabust }	*The Baldwin Family*
Margaret Stahl	
Oreste Rallis	*Police Chief*

with the Penegryis, Greek Folk Dance and Songs Society: director, Dora Stratou; artistic and music director, Fivos Anoyanakis; choreographer, Yianni Fleury.

STORY

Diving for sponges off the Greek isle of Hydra, peasant girl Phaedra glimpses a golden statue of a boy mounted upon a dolphin, chained to the hull of a wreck which proves to be 2,000 years old. Together with Rhif her fisherman lover, Niko her little brother and an English medico Dr. Hawkins, she tries to locate a rich American to recover the sunken trove. They have two possibilities: Dr. Jim Calder, a U.S. archaeologist, devoted to returning such finds to governments—and Victor Parmalee, crooked connoisseur, prepared to pay highly to quench his insatiable thirst for antiquities. Rhif eagerly settles for Parmalee's bribe, while Phaedra and Niko slowly understand Calder's approach to national treasures. Ordering Phaedra to keep Calder amused and

Twins. Director Jean Negulesco (below) on the set with Sophia and her stand-in, Scilla Gabel.

Wet look—the pose that launched a thousand shifts.

preoccupied with her dancing, Rhif moves the statue from their hiding-place, ropes it beneath his boat—and ties up Phaedra for good measure—and sails for Parmalee's yacht. Calder alerts the government and young Niko saves the golden boy for posterity. By which time, Calder has eyes for one treasure: Phaedra.

NOTES
Look what Britain missed! According to *Picturegoer*

at the time, Associated British Picture Corporation had been offered the David Divine book and turned it down. Flat. Fox bought it 'for probably ten times the money' and rushed it out into general-release cinemas long before her previous assignment, *The Pride and the Passion*—just as they rushed out Presley's début, *Love Me Tender*—and scooped up all the action emanating from the Italian pin-up and more recent United Artists publicity.

Everyone went a bundle on the wet-again Loren;

Tough guys. Alan Ladd was dwarfed in every way by Loren; Jorge Mistral struck a loftier stance.

Time magazine could not stop frothing. '... the great moment of that early phase of her career came when she played a sponge diver in *Boy on a Dolphin*. Following the custom of the native girls in the Greek islands, she lifted her skirt towards her hips, tucked it between her legs and pinned it back to her belt. She dived into the mottled blue-green Aegean and when she came up, all dripping and skin-soaked, the sea had yielded its finest vision since Botticelli painted Aphrodite on her shell.'

'A film you can't afford to miss,' raved *The People*.

'Sophia the gorgeous ... sultry, sexy ... a Vesuvius of a beauty,' yelled the *Daily Herald*. 'This lusty Loren girl is going to scare the living daylights out of Jayne Mansfield, Marilyn Monroe and Ava Gardner,' prophesied the *Daily Express*. *Monthly Film Bulletin*, as usual, stayed closer to terra firma: 'Sophia Loren has not yet mastered either the English language or the technique of film acting.'

Double. With Hollywood dollars at stake, Sophia was too precious to risk under the Aegean. Scilla Gabel was her 'swim-in'.

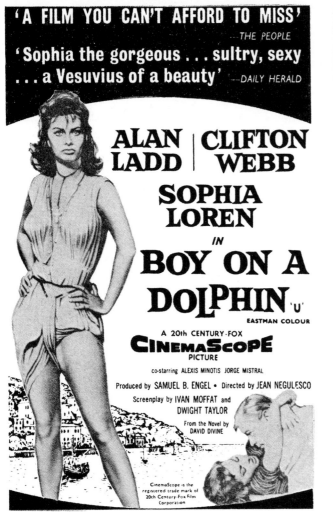

Publicity. Posters trimmed the Loren figure—but not her
allure.

Legend Of The Lost

1957

American-Panamanian/Italian. United Artists. Batjac Productions/Panama Inc./Dear Film (Rome) co-production. *Director/Producer:* Henry Hathaway. *Associate Producer:* Robert Haggiag. *Script:* Robert Presnell Jr., Ben Hecht. *Photography:* Jack Cardiff. *Editor:* Bert Bates. *Music:* A. F. Lavagnino. *Art Director:* Alfred Ybarra. *Sound:* John Keen, W. H. Milner. Technirama. Technicolor. 108 minutes.

CAST

John Wayne . . . . *Joe January*
Sophia Loren . . . . *Dita*
Rossano Brazzi . . . . *Paul Bonnard*
Kurt Kaznar . . . . *Prefect Dukas*
Sonia Moser, Angela Portaluri. . . . *Girls*
Ibrahim El Hadish . . . . *Galli Galli*

STORY

Paul Bonnard hires top desert guide Joe January to take him into the Sahara to an immense treasure in a lost city discovered by Paul's missionary father. *En route* they are joined against Joe's will by Dita, a ravishing slave girl: 'two men and a dame put a strain on any civilisation'. Conquering blistering sand storms, hostile Taureg natives, tarantulas and the more personal obstacle of rivalry between both men for the girl, they reach the ruins of Timgad in bad shape. Paul gets worse, close to insanity, on finding both gold and proof of his worshipped father's unsavoury past—he tries to assault Dita and kill Joe, then disappears with the supplies. Surviving on a tin of peaches and a solitary donkey, Joe and Dita trek back and find the heat-crazed Paul. As Joe digs for water, Paul stabs him—Dita has to shoot him dead. Alone in the flaming sands, with little more than faith in their new-found love, Joe and Dita seem bound to die of thirst when a camel caravan headed back to Timbuktu rescues them.

NOTES

A memorable encounter. Sophia, man-handled waif of the Timbuktu gutter—'I hate men'—meets Wayne, tarnished old hand of the Sahara: 'And I hate loud chippies!' Off-screen, the Duke's appraisal of the new wonder-girl was more laudatory. 'She's been bitten by scorpions, marooned in sandstorms, but nothing can stop that gal. She makes all us men

The Duke. After standing in ditches to accommodate Alan Ladd's lack of height, Loren found a man of her own size—big John Wayne.

look like ninnies. I came here to find hidden treasure and I've found a goldmine. When she gets to Hollywood, she'll slay them!'
Picturegoer: 'The film is a full-blown tribute to the full-blown charms of Loren. There's a plot of sorts. A do-gooder (Brazzi) lands up in Timbuktu with a mission. He wants to cross the Sahara to find the lost city and treasure that obsessed his father ... Well, what with Sophia being built the way she is and wearing a dress that's torn in all the interesting places, you can safely bet that civilisation won't approve of events to come.'
Evening Standard: 'A film in search of its audience. With box-office takings down and a cold wind blowing through the studios, it peddles its hokum like oven-hot corn ... always looks good even when it sounds silly. The question is: will the public go for the old flavour? ... Sophia has the habit of leaving the top buttons of her dress undone and by the

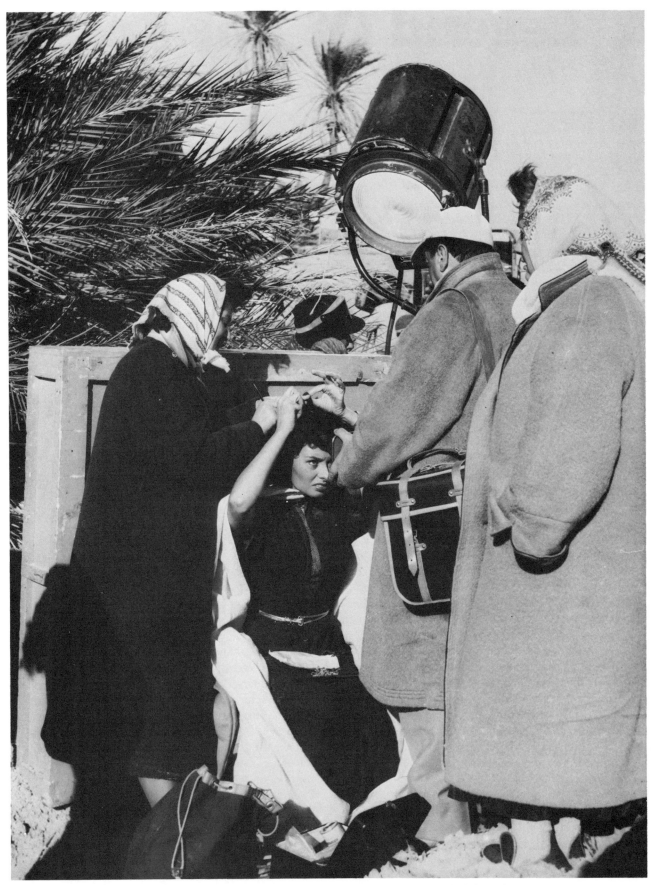

Location. Even a Timbuktu gutter-girl has to have her hair in order.

Smitten. 'Duke' Wayne took the word back to Hollywood: a 'goldmine' was coming.

time the treasure is found, Brazzi discovers that abstinence makes the heart grow fonder.'

Monthly Film Bulletin: 'Not even Jack Cardiff's photography is any compensation for this flimsy and tediously protracted yarn. Hathaway parodies his old liking for brutality and the three stars are most likeable when cheerfully navigating the main absurdities of dialogue and situation.'

After standing in Greek ditches opposite the tiny Alan Ladd, things were beginning to look up for Loren. 'At last,' she said of Wayne, 'I'm playing with an actor who is my own size.' And Hollywood —next stop—was making ready for the brunette bombshell. No less a rival than Jane Russell, for instance, had seen the coming light—and quickly turned blonde for her own production of *The Fuzzy Pink Nightgown*. The decks were being cleared for action …

Travel. Today Libya—tomorrow Bel Air.

Desire Under The Elms

1958

American. Paramount. *Director:* Delbert Mann. *Producer:* Don Hartman. *Script:* Irwin Shaw—*from the play by* Eugene O'Neill. *Photography:* Daniel Fapp. *Editor:* George Boemler. *Music:* Elmer Bernstein. *Art Directors:* Hal Pereira, Joseph Macmillan Johnson. *Sound:* Harold Lewis, Winston Leverett. Vista-Vision. 111 minutes.

CAST
Sophia Loren . . . . *Anna*
Anthony Perkins . . . . *Eben*
Burl Ives . . . . *Ephraim*
Frank Overton . . . . *Simon*
Pernell Roberts . . . . *Peter*
Anne Seymour . . . . *Eben's Mother*
Greta Granstedt . . . . *Min*
Jean Welles . . . . *Florence*
Rebecca Wells . . . . *Lucinda*

STORY
Eben Cabot vows to attain his rightful inheritance: his father's money and the small New England farm that was his mother's before the flinty old Ephraim worked her to death. After Ephraim's second wife dies, Eben buys out the shares of his two step-brothers in the farm. Ephraim brings home a third bride: Anna is beautiful, Italian and much younger than the 'three score years and ten and tough as hickory' old-timer. She has wed only to gain a home of her own and soon uses her persuasive wiles on Eben to forgo his rights. His refusal is adamant. Anna turns, instead, to Ephraim, promising a son in exchange for the farm. He agrees. But it is Eben who sires the child—unable to resist the mounting passion between Anna and himself. Celebrating the birth, Ephraim reveals his deal with Anna, and bitterly disillusioned, the boy prepares to quit. Anna is grief-stricken and proves her love for Eben the only way she knows how, by smothering their baby to death. Filled with incredulous fury, Eben goes for the sheriff. Anna confesses all to Ephraim, whose wrath falls on his son for deserting her. Eben returns, falls at his lover's feet, begs forgiveness and says he will share her punishment as well as her guilt. Together, they go into custody with the sheriff.

NOTES
At last—the Hollywood début. Sophia's dreams and Ponti's planning come to fruition. And not a bucket

New fields. Hollywood calls. At last.

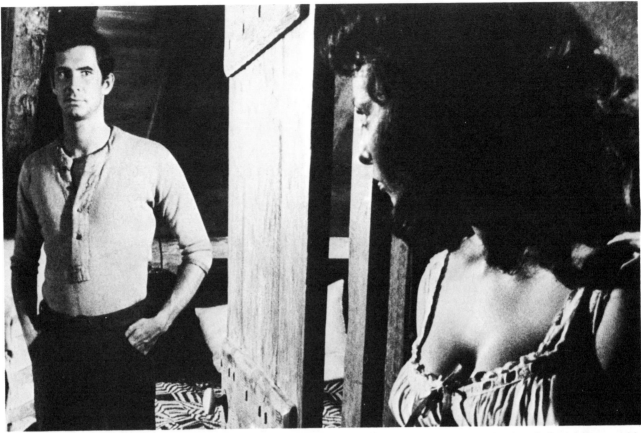

Début. Hollywood style. Loren burns as O'Neill's tragic heroine, snared between an old husband, Burl Ives, and his vengeful son, Anthony Perkins.

of water in sight. The task, however, was nearly beyond her. Too soon, far too early for the girl struggling manfully with English, to tackle such a melodramatic characterisation as O'Neill's tragic Anna. She did not fail, let herself or her backers down, but she did not exactly succeed, either. And yet it was there for all—or at least for De Sica—to see, that glimmer of the Oscar-winning actress-to-be within just three more years.

Bosley Crowther, *New York Times*: '... a strong performance in the rôle of the crafty and passion-charged woman who makes for trouble down on the farm. Even though she is shown as Italian and not the New Englander of the play, she is plausibly in the spirit of the tempestuous drama that unfolds. She is initially the spitfire who can tempt the wild young man with cogent wiles. Then she dissolves into a woman who is raptly and recklessly in love.'

Stanley Kaufman, *The New Republic*: 'The best work is done by Sophia Loren ... breath-stoppingly beautiful, is quite convincing as a woman who has been used harshly by men and who needs to be revenged on the world through this marriage and who is confounded by falling in love.'

Houseboat

1958

American. Paramount-Scribe production. *Director:* Melville Shavelson. *Producer:* Jack Rose. *Script:* Melville Shavelson, Jack Rose. *Photography:* Ray June; *second unit:* Wallace Kelley. *Editor:* Frank Fracht. *Music:* George Dunning. *Art Directors:* Hal Pereira, John Goodman. *Sound:* Hugo and Charles Grenzbach. *Songs:* 'Almost In Your Arms', 'Bing, Bang, Bong' *by* Jay Livingstone and Ray Evans, *sung by* Sam Cooke. VistaVision. Technicolor. 110 minutes.

Duet. The proud and the passionate.

CAST

Cary Grant	*Tom Winston*
Sophia Loren	*Cinzia Zaccardi*
Martha Hyer	*Carolyn Gibson*
Harry Guardino	*Angela Donatello*
Eduardo Ciannelli	*Arturo Zaccardi*
Murray Hamilton	*Alan Wilson*
Mimi Gibson	*Elizabeth Winston*
Paul Peterson	*David Winston*
Charles Herbert	*Robert Winston*
Madge Kennedy	*Mrs. Farmsworth*
John Litel	*Mr. Farmsworth*
Werner Klemperer	*Harold Melsner*

STORY

Aghast at the way his three children are shared out among relatives after their mother's death, Tom Winston hustles the protesting brood from the spaciousness of the Virginia countryside to his cramped Washington flat. Relations are not good. The kids are strangers to him and they resent his pomposity. Robert, the youngest, flees the coop and, after a delicious night out, is returned by Cinzia, a bored socialite with much in common with the lad. She, too, has fled Daddy, orchestral conductor Arturo Zaccardi. Robert blackmails Tom into engaging Cinzia as a maid and eventually the quintet set up home in a ramshackle houseboat. Tom finds Cinzia's presence disconcerting to say the least; gradually he falls for the way she brings understanding to his kids and holds her own with the local country-club snobs. Marriage is in the air. The kids are against it. But good sense will out—likewise Cinzia's father— and the wedding takes place in a noisy atmosphere of reconciliation.

NOTES

'A spirited Sophia Loren,' noted Peter John Dyer in *Monthly Film Bulletin*, 'occasionally breaking into song and dance, seems more at home than in any of her previous American films.' The reason was Cary Grant. Thus far, he alone of the Hollywoodians queueing up for the pin-up/cover-girl sensation, knew her well enough, long enough, to catch the exact lively spirit of Sophia. Her usual radiance was even more enhanced by the news that she had been married, by proxy, in Mexico to Carlo Ponti.

Joyous. Cary Grant showed Hollywood the best side of
Loren—joyful comedienne.

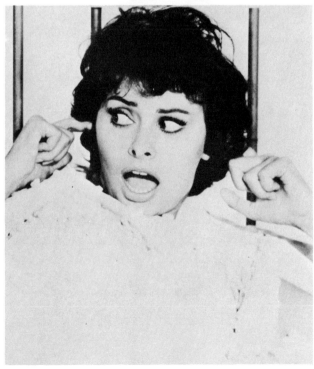

Consummate. Grant the polished pro.; Loren the willing pupil. Her every glance was charged with electric admiration for his effortless elan.

Bride. During shooting, Sophia and Carlo wed by proxy in Mexico.

The Key

1958

British. Columbia Pictures. Open Road production. *Director:* Carol Reed. *Producer:* Aubrey Baring. *Executive Producer/Script:* Carl Foreman—*from the novel* Stella *by* Jan de Hartog. *Photography:* Oswald Morris. *Editor:* Bert Bates. *Music/Conductor:* Malcolm Arnold. *Production Design:* Wilfred Shingleton. *Art Director:* Geoffrey Drake. *Wardrobe:* Bill Walsh, Eileen Welch. *Make-Up:* Dave Aylott. *Hairstyles:* Barbara Ritchie. *Sound:* Peter Handford, W. Milner. *Special Effects:* Willis Cook. *Asst. Director:* Gerry O'Hara. *Royal Navy Technical Advisers:* Capt. J. Broom, Cdr. O. Peake, Cdr. N. Hunter, Cdr. M. Paynter. *Production Manager:* Cecil P. Ford. CinemaScope. 134 minutes.

CAST

William Holden . . . . *David Ross*
Sophia Loren . . . . *Stella*
Trevor Howard . . . . *Chris Ford*
Oscar Homolka . . . . *Capt. Van Dam*
Kieron Moore . . . . *Kane*
Bernard Lee . . . . *Wadlow*
Beatrix Lehmann . . . . *Housekeeper*
Noel Purcell . . . . *Hotel Porter*
Bryan Forbes . . . . *Weaver*
Sidney Vivian . . . . *Grogan*
Rupert Davies . . . . *Baker*
Russell Waters . . . . *Sparks*
Irene Handl . . . . *Clerk*
John Crawford . . . . *U.S. Captain*
Jameson Clark . . . . *British Captain*

STORY

Ex-tugboat man David Ross is co-opted from the Canadian navy during the war to command an ocean-going tug on convoy rescue duty in the Western Approaches. He gets an immediate hint of the mental and physical strain involved from veteran salt Chris Ford. Old friends, Ford invites Ross back to see his little Plymouth flat and the girl that comes with it: Stella, a Swiss refugee. Ford explains that since her skipper-fiancé was killed in action, she has stayed on as lover to a succession of tug-captains, each passing his spare key to a friend before his final voyage:

Decision. Ponti says Sophia made *The Key* against his wishes; director Sir Carol Reed remains delighted that she did.

War relief. Trevor Howard explains life with Stella to William Holden.

Love. Holden inherits Loren—and his part from Henry Fonda.

'Sometimes, old boy, I don't think she knows one of us from the others.' Ford is called to a burning ship, gives his key to Ross 'just in case'. Kane brings dire news: Ford was shot in the chest by strafing German planes. Reluctantly, Ross takes over flat and girl. Soon he feels theirs is a special love, immune to the fate of the others; and she, for the first time, ceases to see her dead fiancé in the owner of the key. A series of coincidences makes Ross believe his number is coming up, he hands his key to Kane—but survives the trip and returns to find Kane already installed. Furious at this betrayal, Stella angrily drives him away and leaves for London. 'I'll find her,' says Ross, 'when I go to London ...'

NOTES
The British début ... and it was entirely Sophia's decision. 'I was against her accepting a part in *The Key*,' admits Ponti. 'But she wanted it, went ahead, signed the contract and the film was made. As it turned out, she showed better judgement than I.' So did Carl Foreman who wanted Loren from the outset: 'I had in mind an ethereal person with a slight, not clearly identifiable accent—an elusive

personality, rather than one which most star actresses have already formed in the minds of their fans.'

For some time, however, it seemed that due to Ponti's mounting Hollywood schedule, neither star nor creator would have their way. Foreman made a private decision that pinpointed the importance of Loren even with such a minor total of English-speaking films to her credit: if he could not obtain Loren, he would go for Ingrid Bergman.

Sophia does not recall Ponti being so much against the film. 'I think they signed me and then thought it was not the rôle for me. They had in mind somebody else and, for the first time in my life, I stamp my foot down and said: "No, you are going to take me because I am going to be good. You have never seen me in a rôle like this, that's why you talk like that." Oh, I was very young then and it was hard to do that, convince them. Finally I won. When the picture came out, the only person everybody mentioned was me. I say that particularly for this film, because it was something I cared about and I was right.'

Director Carol Reed was well pleased with Foreman's choice. 'What struck me was something terribly important to a director. She trusts you right from the start. She gives herself to you as an artist. During shooting, she'd ask me "What did I do wrong? What can I do to make it better?" I never knew her pull an act—the headache, the temperament. Usually with such a beauty, there is worry about the looks. She doesn't bother about looks. She's interested in acting.' (Reed's previous assignment had been *Trapeze* with the old arch-rival, Lollobrigida.)

Foreman wanted to film the de Hartog book for much the same reason as he had written *High Noon*: 'it showed a man alone with fear'. According to Loren, William Holden was perfectly cast. She remembers him full of self-doubts. 'When viewing rushes, he leaves the projection room before the lights go on, because he can't stand the critical reaction of others. For me he made a gallant exception. He stayed and said: "Sophia, you've really got it!"'

King Baudouin of the Belgians told her much the same when the film opened the Brussels World Fair film festival shortly after the world premiere before Princess Margaret in London—when Felix Barker, *Evening News*, hailed it as 'one of the finest films ever produced in this country'. For Columbia, it was the pride of their silver anniversary year.

Monthly Film Bulletin: 'Sophia Loren has not been coaxed into giving more than a token rendering of her lines, although her part is admittedly the most difficult and remains in spite of every attempt on the part of the script to give her a reality of family and background, the most obscurely motivated and mysteriously underwritten.'

Leonard Mosley, *Daily Express*: 'And from Sophia

Missing from cast and screen: Carl Mohner played De Broger, first lover of Stella and owner of the key; featured in the film's opening sequence, he was cut for time on agreement by Foreman and Reed.

Loren, the director has drawn a performance that is touching and tender. She has never looked lovelier, which is no mean achievement when you remember that she is hardly ever seen in anything except her night clothes. In the hands of a less talented actress, this could have been just another story of a kind-hearted woman in a back bedroom. Miss Loren gives the rôle an extra dimension and lifts it above tawdry origins. She helps make *The Key* a strange, sombre, compelling film.'

My question remains the same from 1958: a *Swiss* refugee?

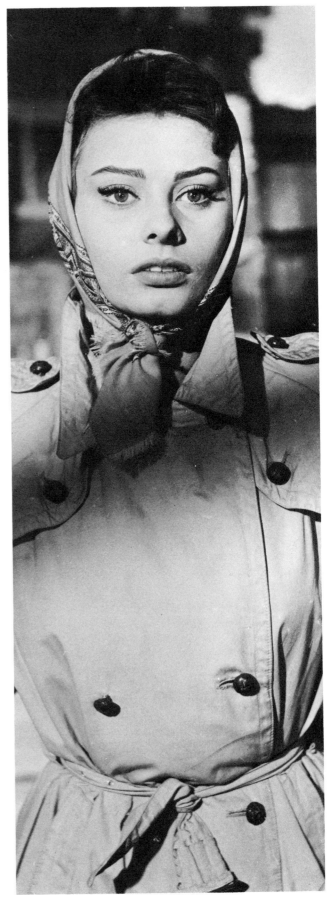

Favourite. *The Key* is one of Sophia's most cherished films. 'I adore it very much.' Her performance stunned critics.

Black Orchid

1959

American. Paramount. Ponti-Girosi production. *Director:* Martin Ritt. *Producers:* Carlo Ponti, Marcello Girosi. *Script:* Joseph Stefano. *Photography:* Robert Burks. *Editor:* Howard Smith. *Music:* Alessandro Cicognini. *Art Directors:* Hal Pereira, Roland Anderson. *Sound:* Hugo Grenzbach, Winston Leverett. VistaVision. 96 minutes.

CAST
Sophia Loren . . . . *Rose Bianco*
Anthony Quinn . . . . *Frank Valente*
Ina Balin . . . . *Mary Valente*
Jimmy Baird . . . . *Ralphie Bianco*
Mark Richman . . . . *Noble*
Naomi Stevens . . . . *Giulia Gallo*
Virginia Stevens . . . . *Alma Gallo*
Joe Di Reda . . . . *Joe*
Frank Puglia . . . . *Henry Gallo*

STORY
Rose Bianco blames herself for her husband's death. An Italian living in New York's poor quarter, she longed for luxuries and he provided—at the cost of his life—by becoming a gangster. Now her young son, Ralphie, is confined on a state farm for delinquents and Rose earns a sparse livelihood making artificial flowers. Slowly, widower Frank Valente wins her confidence and love, and that of Ralphie during farm-visits. Frank's daughter, Mary, is not so easy. Her hostility towards Rose reaches pathological proportions when she realises her father is talking marriage. Mary locks herself in her room for days on end and Rose gives up all hope of both marrying Frank and giving Ralphie his promised chance of freedom and family life. Feeling betrayed by events, Ralphie breaks out of the farm. Frank finds him and is returning him as Rose makes a final stab at making Mary see reason. Rose succeeds and her happiness is made complete by marriage to Frank and Ralphie's release into their custody.

NOTES
Hollywood—Italian style. Stage two of the big Hollywood push was controlled completely by Ponti

Reunion. Anthony Quinn meets the starlet from *Attila*— making it big in Hollywood.

Visitors. Loren takes Quinn to meet her son at the delinquents' farm.

and his new partner, Marcello Girosi, producer of *The Sign of Venus* and *Scandal in Sorrento*. In all they had lined up four properties in a Paramount deal, and this was the reason Ponti had not wanted his star locked into *The Key*. He and she, therefore, were preparing to take on the movie capital—their way.

Financially, they failed. Box-office receipts, in the United States at least, did not break records. Artistically, and this surely is what Loren was really into, the potentiality of her talent increased over and over again. And for *Black Orchid*, Sophia ran off with the Best Actress award at the Venice festival. The seeds, then, were being sown. The harvest was about to be ripe. Very ripe indeed. She had already come a long, long way from when first working with Quinn in *Attila the Hun*; so had he, with two Oscars in four years. He proved to be her only leading man of any substance and clout in her Hollywood adventure. 'I adore him,' says Sophia, 'a wonderful actor to work with—but I don't think people like to see us together. Every picture we make, the people didn't seem to like it. *Black Orchid* was the only one that did well. It's very odd because theoretically we could look well together. But no, they don't seem to like us as a team at all.'

Peter John Dyer, *Monthly Film Bulletin*: '... a lightly confected romance ... Sophia Loren mercifully makes nonsense of the film's misleading title.'

Release. Widow's weeds cause a joke on the set.

Conflict. The couple's wedding plans are upset by Quinn's daughter, Ina Balin.

Wedding. Marriage, Little Italy style-cum Hollywood style, as Loren married Frank Valente.

101

That Kind Of Woman

1959

American. Paramount. Ponti-Girosi production. *Director:* Sidney Lumet. *Producer:* Carlo Ponti. *Associate Producer:* Ray Wander. *Script:* Walter Bernstein—*from a story by* Robert Lowry. *Photography:* Boris Kaufman. *Editor:* Howard Smith. *Music:* Daniele Amfitheatrof. *Art Directors:* Hal Pereira, Roland Anderson. *Sound:* James Gleason, Charles Grenzbach. VistaVision. 92 minutes.

CAST

Sophia Loren . . . . *Kay*
Tab Hunter . . . . *Red*
George Sanders . . . . *The Man*
Jack Warden . . . . *Kelly*
Barbara Nichols . . . . *Jane*
Keenan Wynn . . . . *Harry*

STORY

1944. Public Relations man Harry Corwin works for an anonymous millionaire power behind the Pentagon, winning his plush wartime contracts by peddling influence in the form of a ready supply of mistresses to generals and admirals. Harry's current orders from the boss: to take Kay, a stunning brunette, and Jane, blonde and brassy, from Miami to New York, for all the usual reasons. The train is

packed with rowdy G.I.s, including Red, a young paratrooper on embarkation leave. Kay finds it easy and enjoyable to relax with the soldiers and spends the night with Red—lightly dismissing him next morning as the train pulls in. Red is not so simply cut adrift: Jane has been typically indiscreet when romping with Red's pal, Kelly, and the G.I.s are able to pursue the girls to their master's mansion. Seeing the boy is in love with her, that Kay may be lost to his team, the millionaire offers marriage himself. Kay decides between her present life-style luxury and the love she would enjoy with the impecunious and much younger paratrooper, and flees to the rail station again—to join Red on his leave with his folks.

NOTES

With *Houseboat*, this is the best of Sophia's Stateside output. Her light was released from her tight Hollywood bustle and she sparkled throughout— even during the ridiculous climax. The film is also notable as here was her first English-speaking character minus the inevitable final vowel to the name. In much the same fashion as British screen-writers had to come up with possible (often risible) reasons why Americans were in British war films and the like, Loren story-tailors provided get-out excuses for her accent. If not Italian, she had to be 'foreign' and went through a succession of final-vowel handles for her characters: Juana, Phaedra, Dita, Anna, Cinzia, Stella, Rose to date, heaps more

Party. Joy girls Sophia Loren and Barbara Nichols live it up on the train with GI's Jack Warden and Tab Hunter. Sidney Lumet directed and it remains among her best Hollywood projects.

Swop. Sophia gives up her 'business' life with George Sanders for true love with Tab Hunter. Remarkably, she made it seem believable ...

to follow. On this occasion, however, no one bothered—and no critic or fan questioned it—as the star's luminous sophistication carried off a thoroughly unbelievable rôle to glorious perfection.

Sticking to what they felt were Euro-minded American directors, the Ponti-Girosi team showed foresight, if not enough aft-sight, in selecting Sidney Lumet to direct. One of the brightest TV graduates, he tended to avoid Hollywood—and Hollywoodisms. As with his first two films (*Twelve Angry Men* and *Stage Struck*) he shot the movie completely in New York; sadly it was edited, or much re-edited, back in Hollywood, which explains the distinct unevenness. 'It was a totally romantic piece and treated as such,' said Lumet. 'The problems there were studio problems. Ponti and I didn't get along.'

Robin Bean, *Films and Filming*: '... Sophia Loren giving the best performance of her American-made films. The story was simple, in romantic terms ... Sophia is left with the choice between honest love and wealth. But it was surprisingly witty, well-controlled and avoided all the old sentimental clichés.'

Peter John Dyer, *Monthly Film Bulletin*: 'Despite tactful direction, Tab Hunter's odd moments of genuine pathos and his single hypnotised expression of boyish idealism hardly match up to Sophia Loren's flexible and extremely sophisticated technique. Consequently, their final reunion, far from being the touching moment intended, irreverently puts one in mind of nothing so much as a sea-scout given a luxury liner for Christmas.'

Heller In Pink Tights

1960

American. Paramount. Ponti-Girosi production. *Director:* George Cukor. *Producers:* Carlo Ponti, Marcello Girosi. *Script:* Dudley Nichols, Walter Bernstein—*from a story by* Louis L'Amour. *Photography:* Harold Lipstein. *Colour Co-ordination:* Hoyningen-Huene. *Editor:* Howard Smith. *Music:* Daniele Amfitheatrof. *Art Directors:* Hal Pereira, Eugene Allen. *Décor:* Sam Comer, Grace Gregory. *Sound:* John Wilkinson, Winston Leverett. *Second Unit: director,* Arthur Rossen; *photography,* Irving Roberts. Technicolor. 100 minutes.

CAST

Sophia Loren	*Angela Rossini*
Anthony Quinn	*Tom Healy*
Steve Forrest	*Clint Mabry*
Eileen Heckart	*Lorna Hathaway*
Margaret O'Brien	*Della Southby*
Edmund Lowe	*Manfred 'Doc' Montague*
Ramon Navarro	*De Leon*
George Matthews	*Sam Pierce*
Cactus McPeters	*William*
Frank Cordell	*Theodore*

STORY

The West, *circa* 1880. The Healy Dramatic Company is on tour—one jump ahead of a long line of sheriffs. Their top star, Angela Rossini, has a taste for finery and a habit of running up debts. Hoping to settle in Cheyenne, they begin rehearsals for a spirited production of *Mazeppa*. Angie experiments with poker, runs out of money (again) and stakes herself on a hand. She loses (again)—to gunfighter Clint Mabry. With more credits on the horizon, the troupe make off (again) and Mabry strings along to keep an eye on his winnings. He saves them from an Indian attack and, once they reach safety, Healy is incensed to hear about the poker game. Angie rides off with Mabry to Bonanza, where he is owed money by the treacherous town boss, De Leon. She secures the money and promptly blows it on transforming an old building into The Healy Theatre. The troupe catch up with them; *Mazeppa* is in rehearsal (again). Healy and Angie clear their consciences (again) by both helping Mabry escape De Leon's gunmen and repaying his money. The Healy Dramatic Company seem to have a permanent home. (Again.)

NOTES

Cinderella continues to fulfil her dreams. Twofold here. A Western, the goal of many a European star raised on them in their childhood—and Cukor directing, acknowledged to be the finest actresses' director in the United States. And a blonde wig to boot. Not all dreams are sweet. Here was another Hollywood flop—and the last. Cukor-critics, however, adored it; they would.

Cukor told *Sight and Sound*: 'A film which lent itself to colour treatment and it was very much Hoyningen-Huene's work. Visually and in the performances it was very diverting, even if it wasn't a very good story, and it annoyed me that the picture was passed over so lightly in America. Paramount had no real faith in it, they did some stupid cutting, then it wasn't even released properly. It's a great pity, because amongst other things it seemed to me a very interesting view of the West. I believe

Inevitable. Hollywood just *had* to turn her blonde.

Mummers. Quinn and Loren in a spirited version of *Mazeppa*. Their third film together and yet she feels they're not enjoyed as a screen team.

Poker. Sophia is the pot—and Steve Forrest wins all.

that the West really did look like that.' And to Gavin Lambert he added: 'I thought Sophia Loren very good, light and humorous. She's really adorable.'

Monthly Film Bulletin: 'Part Western, part theatrical comedy, and is made with a gay and sometimes entrancing feeling for the background of barn-like theatres, wagons loaded down with stage finery, rehearsals of 19th-century success in the frontier towns. George Cukor, a director who has not lately been very lucky in his subjects, has clearly responded to this one and the company, notably a blonde Sophia Loren, Margaret O'Brien as a reluctant ingénue and Eileen Heckart as the defiant old trouper, have responded to him. The film's handicap is its plot ... [but] has a welcome individuality which is never entirely smothered by these lapses in convention.'

And so, after five films in America in a couple of years, Loren and Ponti said farewell to Hollywood. Never to return. At least, they have not yet. 'It is not their fault that they did not know what to do with me. To the Americans, we Italians are still mostly gangsters and waiters. And they have never been able to accept a foreign actress for what she is. They feel they must change her. So it was with me. Had I stayed on I would have become just another assembly line beauty. That's why I came home ...'

Bosley Crowther, *New York Times*: 'Patrons familiar with theatre and American theatrical lore may note in Sophia Loren's characterisation as a tempestuous member of a hard-luck troupe, a slight resemblance to Adah Isaacs Menken, who was a favourite of the frontier towns in her flashy performance of *Mazeppa* lashed to the back of a horse. Miss Loren, shapely in pink tights and sapine upon a ponderous nag, may be a bit more chic than was Miss Menken, but the implication is there ... Miss Loren is remarkably appealing, as warm and natural as she has been in anything since that little pizza item in *Gold of Naples.*'

It Started In Naples

1960

American. Paramount. Capri production. *Director:* Melville Shavelson. *Producer:* Jack Rose. *Script:* Melville Shavelson, Jack Rose, Suso Cecchi d'Amico —*from a story by* Michael Pertwee and Jack Davies. *Photography:* Robert L. Surtees. *Colour Consultant:* Hoyningen-Huene. *Editor:* Frank Bracht. *Music:* Alessandro Cicognini, Carlo Savino. *Art Directors:* Hal Pereira, Roland Anderson. *Sound:* Sash Fisher, Charles Grenzbach. VistaVision. Technicolor. 100 minutes.

CAST

Clark Gable . . . . *Mike Hamilton*
Sophia Loren . . . . *Lucia Curcio*
Marietto . . . . *Nando*
Vittorio De Sica . . . . *Mario Vitale*
Paolo Carlini . . . . *Renzo*
Claudio Ermelli . . . . *Luigi*
Giovanni Filidoro . . . . *Gennariello*

Resuscitation. Back to Napoli—and she's a new woman, the old magic gloss blotting out Hollywood's garish tinsel.

STORY

Further adventures of the ugly (don't-drink-the-water) American in Europe.... Sedate Philadelphia lawyer Michael Hamilton arrives in Naples to settle his dead brother's estate and finds it includes a nephew, the offspring of his brother and the Italian girl killed with him. Nando is ten and looked after by his aunt Lucia, a dazzling night-club dancer on Capri. Nando touts for the club, stays up half the night, smokes cigarettes and indulges in petty theft. Hamilton is aghast and insists on the lad being raised as a regular American. Lucia wants to keep him and the matter is put to the courts. During the tussle for Nando's affections, the couple fall in love and quarrel a lot when Hamilton makes it clear that marriage is out. In court, Hamilton's lawyer, Vitale, is so captivated by Lucia he virtually switches camp. Victory for Lucia! Except by this time she suspects an American upbringing may be best for the boy. Pretending she is bored with him, she drives him to Hamilton. He, too, has had second thoughts and sends the boy packing and follows him to Lucia. The ugly American capitulates. The future will be irresponsible but it will not be dull!

NOTES

What better place to lick Hollywood wounds, than back in the invigorating atmospherics and sun-drenched embrace of Naples. The *Houseboat* team, Shavelson and Rose, supplied an impeccably timed gift of a fun-movie, with familiar, trusted colleagues back on company strength: writer d'Amico, composer Cicognini (who lasted for one only of the U.S. movies) and, above all, De Sica co-starring. The overall effect on Sophia—and the film—was gloriously infectious. The Loren limbs jingled, jangled, *lived* again, the vibrancy returned to the entire wondrous body, the smile was no longer painted and the laugh—oh! that laugh—was clearly spontaneous once more. The refugee from the L.A. conveyor-belt was wholly resuscitated by this zesty transplant back home. Well okay, if in the United States, most of them did not know what to do with her, she would stick to *terra firma all'italiana* ... and remain undeniably matchless!

Even the *Monthly Film Bulletin* critics, until now impossible to please, fell to knees in praise. 'That it ends up well on the right side is due mainly to

The King. Virility intact, Clark Gable, the King of Hollywood, met his match—and on her turf.

111

Swim wares. And she owed all she had to ... spaghetti.

Embrace. The new Queen captures the King. But the cigarette (and holder) look out of place ...

Sophia Loren who sings, dances, cooks, quarrels, snaps her fingers and takes off Anna Magnani, all with such good humour and aplomb. The total and not all that usual impression is that the cast enjoyed the comedy themselves.' The *M.F.B.* too!

Variety conceded that 'Gable and Miss Loren are a surprisingly effective and compatible comedy pair'. René Jordan's Gable monograph, though, found it 'an embarrassing throwback to his heyday as an irresistible woman-tamer. In a climactic scene, Loren starts stripping him coquettishly of his tie and jacket while they undulate on a dance floor. He embraces her tightly and the sequence dissolves in a fuzzy, Vaselined close-up of her ecstatic face. The traditional symbolic fade-out indicated Loren had

received the Gable treatment: in the next shot she is seen releasing a dozen balloons into the dawn-lit skies of Capri....'

As well she might. Although raised nearby, Loren had never visited Capri before. 'I was too poor to afford the trip. I would gaze longingly at it glittering on the horizon, an enchantment beckoning, but unattainable. And it was Clark Gable who, knowing every foot of Capri, took me on a tour by carriage....'

Gable's rôle had originally been constructed with our Gracie Fields in mind—while shooting it, he received the script of his next, 66th and last film, *The Misfits.*

Owch! Make-up for a bruised shoulder. Gable handled 'em rough.

Replay. De Sica defends Loren in court; the scene, the pose are almost identical from when he appeared for La Lollo in Blasetti's *Altri Tempi/Times Gone By*, 1952.

A Breath Of Scandal

Olympia

1960

American-Italian-Austrian. Paramount. Titanus (Rome)/Ponti-Girosi/Paramount production. *Director:* Michael Curtiz. *Producers:* Carlo Ponti and Marcello Girosi. *Script:* Walter Bernstein—*from the play* Olympia *by* Ferenc Molnar, *adapted by* Sidney Howard. *Photography:* Mario Montuori. *Editor:* Howard Smith. *Music:* Alessandro Cicognini; *title waltz,* Robert Stolz; *lyric,* Al Stillman. *Art Directors:* Hal Pereira, Eugene Allen. *Song:* 'A Smile in Vienna' *by* Sepp Fellner, Karl Schneider and Patrick Michael; *sung by* Maurice Chevalier. Technicolor. 98 minutes. [No. 2162]

CAST

Sophia Loren . . . . *Princess Olympia*
Maurice Chevalier . . . . *Prince Philip*
John Gavin . . . . *Charlie Foster*
Isabel Jeans . . . . *Princess Eugenie*
Angela Lansbury . . . . *Countess Lina*
Robert Risso . . . . *Aide*
Frederick Ledebar . . . . *Count Sandor*
Carlo Hintermann . . . . *Prince Rupert*
Tullio Carminati . . . . *Albert*
Adrienne Gessner . . . . *Amelia*
Milly Vitale . . . . *Can-Can Girl*

STORY

Vienna, 1905. Exiled to the country for some new scandal, Princess Olympia rushes headlong into another when she meets Pittsburg mining engineer Charlie Foster and spends an innocent night alone with him in a hunting lodge. She forgets him immediately when summoned back to court and told she is to wed Prince Rupert of Prussia. Charlie does not give up, and gatecrashes a party to talk business with her father, Prince Philip. Olympia's rival, Countess Lina, scents another scandal afoot and reports to the Emperor, who dispatches protocol chief Count Sandor to investigate. Charlie promises to keep silent about their initial meeting, if Olympia is allowed by her mother, Princess Eugenie, to spend a weekend with him back at the lodge. After various misunderstandings, Olympia falls in love—and is nonplussed when the rigidly correct Charlie refuses to consummate their passion. In Vienna, the Emperor castigates the jealous Lina, forgives Olympia and allows the marriage to Rupert to go on despite her indiscretions. Olympia elopes instead with Charlie to America.

NOTES

The last of the Ponti-Girosi deal for Paramount; a very damp fuse indeed. Apart from the two films with Anthony Quinn, scant effort had ever been seen to be made by the Ponti team to obtain actors of major substance and virility to draw the fire from Loren. If Tab Hunter could be likened (and was) to a sea-scout, then John Gavin—the second-string Rock Hudson at Universal, and president of the Screen Actors' Guild from 1971—was more akin to a scout camp's tent-pole. Wooden is the polite euphemism for Gavin the thespian, who proves that handsome is, is not the same as handsome does. The most scandalous thing about the entire venture, according to Bosley Crowther, *New York Times,* was the fortune squandered on such a slip of an idea. 'Miss Loren swings through her performance as if she finds much more charm (and why not?) in the loud and lacey costumes than she does in her princess rôle.'

Peter John Dyer, *Monthly Film Bulletin*: '[the film] takes us back to a Nelson Eddy-Jeanette Macdonald world in which impossibly respectable and persistent American commoners in vintage cars triumph over

Regal. As she said in the Lollo feud days, 'She is always going to have trouble playing a *gran signora*, something I have no trouble doing.'

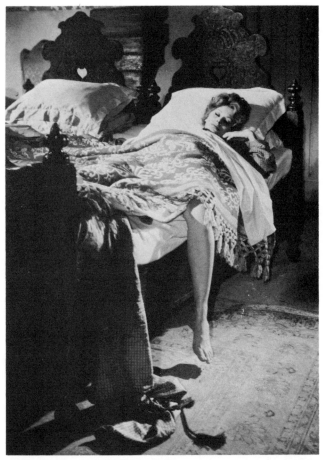

Twist. Olympia was a princess with a touch of the minx about her.

a morally lax European aristocracy by finally winning the hearts of bored and wilful princesses. Sophia Loren and John Gavin lack the sparkle and timing which might still have brought the film to life. But though Gavin is too stiff and though Loren—unsuitably cast, made-up and coiffeured—seems understandably preoccupied, the film has a saving grace in Isabel Jeans' stylish, dominating performance as Olympia's mother.'

Robert Vas, *Sight and Sound*: 'A dispirited Michael Curtiz left the stars to their own devices. This seems specially hard on Sophia Loren, in any case not an ideal choice for a princess, who obviously still needs the help of a Lumet or a Cukor in sharpening the finer points of her comedy technique.'

No sir, what the girl required was De Sica.

Clash. John Gavin, alas, was not up to the occasion, her poorest co-star since Tab Hunter. The wooden was never made flesh.

The Millionairess

1960

British. 20th Century-Fox. Dimitri de Grunwald production. *Director:* Anthony Asquith. *Producer:* Pierre Rouve. *Script:* Wolf Mankowitz—*based on the play by* George Bernard Shaw; *adapted by* Riccardo Aragno. *Photography:* Jack Hildyard. *Editor:* Anthony Harvey. *Music/Conductor:* Georges van Parys. *Production Design:* Paul Sheriff. *Art Director:* Harry White. *Costumes:* Pierre Balmain. *Make-Up:* Dave Aylott. *Hairstyles:* Sarah Beber. *Sound:* Gerry Turner. CinemaScope. Eastmancolor. 90 minutes.

CAST

Sophia Loren . . . . *Epifania Parerga*
Peter Sellers . . . . *Dr. Kabir*
Alastair Sim . . . . *Sagamore*
Vittorio De Sica . . . . *Joe*
Dennis Price . . . . *Adrian*
Gary Raymond . . . . *Alastair*
Alfie Bass . . . . *Fish Curer*
Miriam Karlin . . . . *Mrs. Joe*
Noel Purcell . . . . *Professor*
Virginia Vernon . . . . *Polly*
Basil Hoskins . . . . *Secretary*
Diana Coupland . . . . *Nurse*
Willoughby Goddard . . . . *President*
Pauline Jameson . . . . *Muriel*
Graham Stark . . . . *Butler*
Wally Patch . . . . *Whelk-Seller*

STORY

Epifania Parerga, heiress to her father's industrial empire, and duty-bound to behave as a millionairess should, craves marriage. But she cannot make a man happy. He would need to be as exceptional as she is, says her shrewd solicitor sage, Sagamore. She finds the man: Kabir, a lowly, but highly principled, Indian doctor, running a clinic for the East End poor. She knows it is him. When he touches her (clinically), looks at her (clinically?) and speaks to her (prescriptively). He wants her, too, but is scared of being submerged in her enormous power and will; an example of which is the clinic she builds for him, a colossus of glass and concrete and not an ounce of soul. Kabir puts her off with a tale about promising his mother any girl he would marry would prove herself by earning her living for three months, starting with just £3 6s. and the clothes she stood in. Epifania gives Kabir her father's condition: take £500 and triple it in three months. Epifania cannot miss and Kabir knows he has to fail. With the Parerga magic, she meets an Italian, Joe, and converts his sweat-shop bakery into a modernised production unit geared for maximum profit. Kabir cannot give his money away, much less increase it, and he decides to help Prof. Merton with his cold cure hunt. The triumphant Epifania is crushed at Kabir's failure, resigns her wealth and prepares to open a nunnery in Tibet ... until the wily Sagamore prevents complete disaster and the end of his percentage.

NOTES

In which Cinderella extends her largesse ... Nobody, but nobody (as the saying went in 1960) would have dared thought of teaming Sophia and Sellers in any kind of film venture, much less an adaptation of

Visitation. Dr. Sellers finds his sick-call remarkably fit.

Shaw, despite their considerable individual successes in the '50s. Loren was now well out of the old horizontal-vertical school, having demonstrated her talents were more than anatomical in both Hollywood and European projects; while Sellers, the multi-faced-and-voiced goon who had started his screen career as the off-screen voices of a parrot and Churchill, had displayed acting prowess beyond mere mimicry and collected a British Oscar in *I'm All Right Jack* in 1959. Until now, however, his sexiest co-stars had been Katie Johnson and Margaret Rutherford—aged 75 and 65 respectively! Dimitri de Grunwald and 'Puffin' Asquith thought more adventurously and the deal was made—just as Sellers' clairvoyant told him it would be: 'An African or Indian rôle opposite a tall, dark and very good-looking woman ... connected in its early stages with water.' Sellers' first scene was in a rowing boat when Sophia's Epifania stages her deliberate

flop of a suicide bid. And the casting gamble paid off long before the premiere, on the studio floor where the comedy-loving duo got on like the proverbial blazing house. Sophia adored his range of voices, and greatly extended her large repertoire of cockney expressions. For his part, Sellers joined the smitten co-star list and hailed Sophia in words everyone was fully accustomed to when reading of her: 'Magnetic, fantastic—100 per cent woman.' There was talk of further films together (*Madame Sans-Gêne* and maybe *A Shot in the Dark*) and they made a jolly record album of sketches and songs, a single from which, *Goodness, Gracious Me*, based on their G.B.S. rôles, was released to coincide with the picture—which greatly suffered from the lack of it anywhere on the soundtrack.

The film, exactly as Sellers' clairvoyant had predicted, proved to be 'successful in this country but not abroad'. Still, Sellers became an international

Treatment. After examining a patient like La Loren, 'twas the medico's blood-pressure in trouble.

Revelation. Sophia with De Sica—the morning after the £250,000 robbery of her jewels.

Appropriation. The millionairess and her sagacious lawyer, Alastair Sim.

name and Sophia established yet again her command of comedy ... even when shooting the day after the front-page-news robbery of her £250,000 jewellery collection.

Peter John Dyer, *Monthly Film Bulletin*: 'Not content to treat Shaw's play for what it was, an outmoded, rambling, but still intermittently diverting social fantasy on the one hand, and a foolproof actress' vehicle on the other, Asquith has attempted to give new life to the story by peppering it with trick devices (prolonged super-impositions and painful bouts of frenzied cross-cutting) and either extravagantly dressing or persistently undressing his leading actress. Though badly miscast, Sophia Loren is made, quite unforgivably, to look almost amateurish by Asquith's ponderously infatuated direction. She still has an enjoyable game shot at Shaw's juggernaut of a heroine—notably in the scene of her elegant Thameside suicide attempt ... Some of the other expert players are only too plainly uncomfortable ... Indeed, without Sellers, the wreck would

have been virtually complete.'

Bosley Crowther, *New York Times*: 'With the casual air of a showgirl who has no idea what the show is all about—knowing only that she's supposed to model those costumes and generate a miasma of sex-appeal—Miss Loren postures and swivels through virtually every scene she plays ... From the way she performs this lady, it appears her only idea of how to snare the fellow is to run the range of wiles of a vamp. She lies seductively on sofas, takes advantage of the possibilities of low-cut gowns, occasionally slips out of her dresses and when she isn't rolling her hips, she rolls her eyes. The performance is so calculated and so discordant with the drone of Shavian quips ... that it's as if Miss Loren is doing an act all by herself. It is not a very good act and it becomes monotonous.'

Ponti, missing from the production scene on this occasion, was ready to produce an ace from his sleeve ... and have all the critics eating their reviews.

Two Women

La Ciociara

1961

Italo-French. Gala Films (Embassy Pictures Corp. in U.S.). Champion (Rome)/Les Films Marceau-Cocinor/S.G.C. (Paris) co-production. *Director:* Vittorio De Sica. *Producer:* Carlo Ponti. *Script:* Cesare Zavattini—*from the novel by* Alberto Moravia. *Camera:* Mario Capriotti. *Editor:* Adriana Novelli. *Music:* Armando Trovajoli. CinemaScope. 110 minutes (U.K. 100). [No. 2346]

CAST

Sophia Loren . . . . *Cesira*
Eleanora Brown . . . . *Rosetta*
Raf Vallone . . . . *Giovanni*
Jean-Paul Belmondo . . . . *Michele*
Renato Salvatori . . . . *Florindo*

STORY

Italy, 1943. As the bombardment of San Lorenzo increases, young widow Cesira entrusts her small grocery shop to her sometime coalman-lover Giovanni and quits Rome for her native village of Sant'Eufemia in the region of Ciociara, with her 13-year-old daughter. By train, mule and foot, under machine-gun fire from low-flying planes, they reach the village and settle in a small cottage where many of the locals congregate for nightly company. Among them, Michele, a farmer's student son known as The Professor. Rosetta falls for him, but it is Cesira who attracts him. The war gets still closer as the Allies approach, bombing is more frequent and food is scarce. Michele is forced at gun-point to guide some fleeing Germans across the mountains and Cesira decides to move again. Exhausted and dirty, they take refuge in a bombed-out church. Suddenly, from the shadows, mother and daughter are pulled apart and raped by a crowd of yelling Allied Moroccan soldiers. Regaining consciousness, Cesira, in agony, finds the outraged body of her daughter, straightens her clothes and tries to help her forget her traumatic experience. In shock, Rosetta is transformed from girl into woman. Continuing their heart-rending trek back to Rome, they are given a lift by truck-

driver Florindo and a bed overnight at his parents'. Cesira wakes to find Rosetta missing. She returns hours later after dancing with Florindo who has given her a pair of nylon stockings. For Cesira it

Anguish. A mother's despair at the horrendous rape of her teenage daughter and herself. A performance hacked from memory of the faces of a war-torn childhood: faces of hope, anger, love (for daughter Eleanora Brown) and traumatic grief.

seems the end: the daughter she loves above all else is no more. Nothing touches her embittered, young heart ... until Cesira screams the news of Michele's death—and the girl breaks down, clasped in her mother's arms.

NOTES

And so to the zenith ...! Best Actress at the 14th Cannes festival, awards from Cork and the British Film Academy and an Oscar, the first to a foreign actress in a foreign-language film, to join Ponti's for *La Strada*. Plus, needless to say, the critical reviews of her life for the rôle (almost literally) of her life. Beat that, Hollywood! Without a foot wrong, apart from those over-manicured eyebrows, Europe's top female star presented a bravura *tour de force* in the Magnani class. And it was, of course, a project originally planned with Magnani in mind as Cesira, Loren as the daughter—and George Cukor directing! Magnani made it abundantly, repeatedly clear she would never entertain the notion of playing Sophia's mother—and the triumph was sweeter than the champagne it unleashed in Rome.

Headlined reviews ranged from the *Daily Mirror*'s DYNAMITE! to the *Bournemouth Times'* SO FINE, SOPHIA! The *Mirror* likened her uninhibited playing to 500 pin-tables flashing at once and my own review in the more lowly seaside journal questioned the reality of the performance. 'Her superb figure is hidden by shapeless garb, her luscious legs in ugly woollen socks. But her face, although brimming with tears, hatred, occasionally love, never loses the Hollywood gloss. Even after an unnecessary opening romp with a coalman in Rome, all she gets is rather an effective streak on her face ... Sophia tries—and nearly succeeds—in out-Magnani-ing Magnani. To be honest, she'd have been better as the daughter.'

Alexander Walker, *Evening Standard*: 'As Anna Magnani has done in a dozen films, Loren plays a woman who is tough, sardonic, passionate and ready to assuage her widowhood with the man next door, while remaining mindful of her own best interests ... Like Magnani, Loren makes a fiercely protective mother, whose virago tongue conceals the tenderness of a madonna ... On her knees in the roadway, Loren howls out her rage and grief at a convoy passing heedlessly by. At the climax, her motions are scored for brass and she plays them in a way that makes all her past films sound like interludes for seductive flutes.'

Bosley Crowther, *New York Times*: '... the beauty of Miss Loren's performance is in her illumination of a passionate mother rôle. She is happy, expansive, lusty, in the early phases of the film, in tune with the gusto of the peasants, gentle with her child. But when disaster strikes, she is grave and profound.

When she weeps for the innocence of her daughter, one quietly weeps with her.'

Thomas Wiseman, *Sunday Express*: 'It could be said of Anna Magnani that her acting is so good one forgets she is not beautiful. I will pay Sophia Loren the even higher compliment of saying that her acting ... is so good one forgets she is beautiful. It is quite a lot to forget. In previous films, Miss Loren has had to compete against her own scene-stealing natural endowments. One sometimes could not see the acting for the actress. But in this film, looking often as dishevelled as an un-made bed, she gives a performance that a woman-hater—or even another woman—would be compelled to find beautiful.'

One woman certainly did. Penelope Gilliatt's rave tribute to Loren in the *Observer* bemoaned the fact that Britain had no actress to match her fire and sensuality. 'Contrary to the evidence of the society we live in, and with a few treasured exceptions like Billie Whitelaw and Joan Plowright, English film actresses give the impression that their sex as a whole was reared at a Harrod's authors' tea. They could never play Lady Macbeth or Tennessee William's Cat; Moll Flanders would be still harder, and Fanny Hill out of the question. Of irony, recklessness, humour, tenacity, sensual abundance, or moral candour of the exacting sort that many women possess, there is hardly a trace on our screen. Some of what we lack can be summed up in two words: Sophia Loren.'

On the set, De Sica made no bones about his elation. 'You were wonderful!' he exclaimed to Loren. 'You really got into the personality of this woman. These are the rôles in which you give everything you possess. You are an intuitive not a sophisticated woman. Why do you bother playing in America, the elegant women, the woman of the world?'

Sophia refutes the once heavy rumour that Moravia had based his book on the war-time saga of Loren and her Mamina. 'Not at all! People got it all mixed up because I said how much I particularly felt this rôle, that it reminded me of my mother during the war. But Moravia never thought of my mother—he doesn't even know her.

'I never thought the film would be as great as it was. I thought the story very good, what we did every day was good, but this you think always when you do a picture because you believe in what you are doing. When it comes out and hits like *Two Women* did—you *are* surprised. And, of course, I was not expecting the Oscar. If I felt sure of winning, I would have been in Hollywood that night. I was not upset that I wasn't; I was so overwhelmed at being even nominated I think I would have fainted anyway if I had won or not!'

El Cid

1961

American/Italian. Rank Organisation. Samuel Bronston Productions/Dear Film (Rome) co-production. *Director:* Anthony Mann. *Producers:* Samuel Bronston, Robert Haggiag. *Associate Producer:* Michael Waszynski. *Script:* Philip Yordan, Fredric M. Frank. *Photography:* Robert Krasker. *Editor:* Robert Lawrence. *Music:* Miklos Rozsa. *Art Directors/Costumes:* Veniero Colesanti, John Moore. *Make-Up:* Mario Van Riel. *Sound:* Vern Field, Jack Solomon, Gordon K. McCallum. *Second Unit Team: director,* Yakima Canutt; *photography,* Manuel Berenguer. *Special Effects:* Alex Weldone, Jack Erickson. 70 mm Super-Technirama. Technicolor. 185 minutes (U.K. 180).

CAST

Charlton Heston	*Rodrigo Diaz de Bivar*
	—El Cid
Sophia Loren	*Chimene*
John Fraser	*King Alfonso*
Raf Vallone	*Count Ordoñez*
Genevieve Page	*Queen Urraca*
Gary Raymond	*King Sancho*
Herbert Lom	*Ben Yussef*
Massimo Serato	*Fanez*
Douglas Wilmer	*Moutamin*
Frank Thring	*Al Kadir*
Hurd Hatfield	*Count Arias*
Ralph Truman	*King Ferdinand*
Andrew Cruickshank	*Count Gomez*
Michael Hordern	*Don Diego*
Carlo Justini	*Bermudez*
Christopher Rhodes	*Don Martin*
Gerard Tichy	*King Ramirez*
Fausto Tozzi	*Dolfos*
Tullio Carminati	*Priest*
Barbara Everest	*Mother Superior*

STORY

Eleventh-century Spain is divided into Christian kingdoms and Moorish strongholds. The young Rodrigo Diaz de Bivar—dubbed El Seid (The Lord) by a Moor whose life he spares, El Cid by his followers; and the Cid in the movie—vows to see his country at peace, free from the invader. Vigorously brave and resourceful, the noble knight hates bloodshed and faces treason charges at court for the clemency shown to some emirs. His accuser, Gomez, father of his fiancée, Chimene, dies in the resulting duel. Chimene's avowed vengeance plot fails and Rodrigo is given her hand; the marriage is not consummated and she enters a convent. On Ferdinand's death, his kingdom is divided among his three children. Sancho challenges the decision and imprisons Alfonso, who is released by the Cid. The African war-lord, Ben Yussef, takes advantage of the quarrel by having Sancho assassinated. Alfonso now claims that throne, too, and exiles the Cid. Chimene realises the nobility of her husband and joins him, but returns to the convent with their two children, when he goes into battle against Ben Yussef. The years pass, El Cid becomes a revered warrior, but refuses to aid Alfonso, preferring his own strategy.

Action! A smile for Tony Mann, then into the solemn scene.

He lays siege to Valencia, catapulting food into its starving garrison; when the Valencians kill their evil ruler, Al Kadir, they offer the crown to the Cid. He sends it to Alfonso, who rushes, hysterically gratified, to his side. But the Cid has been hit by a stray arrow. Attended by Chimene, he hides the wound from his men and prepares a final bid to drive the Moors from Spain. He will lead his troops, dead or alive; and so his corpse is propped up in his saddle next morning and this seeming immortality panics the enemy. They flee, killing Ben Yussef in their stampede. The battle is won and the name of El Cid passes into legend.

NOTES

. . . and into cinema glory with nary a stain on his saga. (Which, where Americano dollars are concerned, is most unusual to say the least of it.) This is, for my money, the ultimate in the '60s glut of epics, due to Heston, Mann and, of course, Sophia. Plus the most moving, stirring climax ever screened. How could it fail—being set in a time, as Bosley Crowther put it, 'when men were men and women were Sophia Loren'.

Penelope Gilliatt, *Observer*: 'El Cid seems to me one of the most pure and beautiful myths that Hollywood has ever made . . . the most perfectly realised colour picture since Visconti's *Il Senso*. The producer, Samuel Bronston, also produced *King of Kings*, which had about as much religious feeling as a pink plastic crucifix, but the curious thing is that though *El Cid* is not explicitly devout, it is an infinitely more religious film, in the sense that it is a work about a binding rule of life.'

Peter John Dyer, *Monthly Film Bulletin*: '. . . less sickening than *Spartacus*; altogether healthier in its

Boy Scout idealism; it is less likely to offend than *King of Kings*, because Charlton Heston brings to this cardboard knight a stature lacking in Jeffrey Hunter's Christ; it is braver than *Ben-Hur* in that it has to make do with a conventional series of battles for its climax where the other had a pre-sold chariot race (and for that matter, a pre-sold subject) . . . Sophia Loren smoulders in black . . .'

Bosley Crowther, *New York Times*: 'Sophia Loren is lovely, agile and a latent force, little more, as the noble lady who loves him, spurns him and tries to do him in (for honourably killing her father), then is married to him and stands by him to the end.'

Exactly as Anthony Mann knew she would be. If only he could persuade her . . . 'I loved Spain. I

Consumption. The marriage of El Cid and Chimene is consummated as Loren joins Charlton Heston in exile.

Casting coup. From the outset, director Anthony Mann wanted two stars and two stars only: Heston and Loren. Heston was game; Sophia took much persuading. The star who started as a lowly epic-extra won a singular success in a £2,300,000-worth epic of her own.

thought I'd like to do a picture about Spain. Then I read the chronicles and that was the greatest ending I'd ever read—I had to do it. From the beginning I wanted Charlton Heston and Sophia Loren to star. I couldn't visualise anyone else . . . I didn't have any problems in persuading Heston. But Sophia! She was a problem. She didn't want to do the film. Twice she turned it down. I flew to Rome three times and chased her all over the place, but finally she said yes. "I just don't see myself in the part," she said. "But if you say so, I'll try." I don't think she had any idea how relieved I was. You see things were getting desperate. We were almost ready to start and I didn't want to settle for another actress because I knew Sophia would fill it better than anyone. Anyway, she and Heston look so good together. You can't put any actress opposite him. Apart from anything else, he's such a big man. I gambled on getting Loren—and I won.'

He also gambled on the weather, which held up shooting—and lost Peter Sellers his Napoleonic hopes in *Madame*.

Madame

Madame Sans-Gêne

1961

Italo-French-Spanish. Embassy Pictures via 20th Century-Fox. A Gesi/Champion/Cine Alliance (Paris)/Agata (Madrid) production. *Director:* Christian-Jacque. *Producer:* Maleno Malenotti. *Script:* Henri Jeanson, Ennio de Concini, Jean Ferry, Franco Solinas, Christian-Jacque—*from the play by* Emile Moreau, Victorien Sardou. *Photography:* Robert Gerardi. *Editors:* Jacques Desagneaux, Eraldo Da Roma. *Music:* Francesco Lavignino. *Art Directors:* Jean d'Eaubonne, Mario Rappini. *Costumes:* Marcel Escoffier, Itala Scandariato. *Sound:* Ennio Sensi. Technirama. Technicolor. 100 minutes. [No. 2413]

CAST

Sophia Loren . . . . *Catherine Huebscher*
Robert Hossein . . . . *Lefevre*
Julien Bertheau . . . . *Napoleon*
Marina Berti . . . . *Elisa Bonaparte*
Carlo Giuffere . . . . *Jerome*
Gabriella Pallotta . . . . *Héloise*
Amalia Gade . . . . *Caroline*
Laura Valenzuela . . . . *Pauline*
Ginrico Tedeschi . . . . *Roquet*

With Robert Hossein.

STORY

Catherine Huebscher, carefree, outspoken, volatile, is known in her lower-class Paris *quartier* as *Madame Sans-Gêne* (Free and Easy). In 1792, she falls in love with a rugged army sergeant, Lefevre, who has a cannon positioned in her laundry shop. She promises to join him after the revolution which he assures her will last but a few months. Four years later (during which time they meet again once only—to marry) Catherine goes to Napoleon's headquarters to obtain a pass to the front. Bonaparte fails to recognise the girl who did his washing and refuses permission; she goes, anyway, in a wagon-load of camp-followers, finds Lefevre, now a captain, and while seeking privacy they are surrounded and captured by Austrians. They escape and blow up the enemy's ammunition; instead of having Lefevre shot for desertion, Napoleon promotes him colonel. Catherine fights on alongside her man as a *vivandière* in the war and is decorated on the field of battle. Installed as Emperor, Napoleon makes them the Duke and Duchess of Danzig, and soon after Catherine's sumptuously impressive court début, decides to raise them to King and Queen of Westphalia. His sisters are jealous and persuade him such a move would make him the laughing stock of Europe. Napoleon orders Lefevre to divorce and marry a princess. Catherine seems to agree, then visits the Emperor and reminds him of the days he could not pay his laundry bills. Overwhelmed by her, Napoleon decides it better not to separate the couple.

NOTES

As continuing evidence of Loren's vast popularity, not even the hypocritically chauvinistic French objected to her playing *their* heroine. They could not; they had no star of similar robust beauty to better her. To save face, they did supply Hossein's amusing Lefevre ('I was a sergeant, captain, duke—what else could I be next but king?') plus Julien Bertheau's

Gusto. Sophia was a resounding mirth-quake in *Madame*, being the rise and rise of a simple French washer-woman, helping Napoleon and his cannons, following her husband Robert Hossein to war and winding up as Duchess to his Duke of Danzig—with more explosions to come, of gun and face-powder among the troops and the snobbish ladies of court. A ripe, royal, rollicking, ravishing rôle!

Pick-up. Loren as the French heroine, Madame Sans-Gêne, did not worry the chauvinistic French; though Gina Lollobrigida was hardly pleased. Here was yet another project, Loren had taken over when La Lollo dropped out. Although unmentioned at time of shooting, Gina and her husband had originally planned to make the movie—and announced it with Italian film trade paper ads.—in 1960.

thoughtful Napoleon, the rôle once pencilled in for Sellers. A fun-film, more gusto than fire, but when it reached Britain, two years on, one had to contend with more frightful mid-Atlantic dubbing. Sophia did her own and had to reply to: 'Hi, Catherine! You coming with us? We're gonna take the Tuileries!' And live with the Dook of Danzig. She survived. As Bosley Crowther noted, it was a straight vehicle for herself and she rode it luxuriously.

Ian Johnson, *Films and Filming*: 'This is Sophia's film from start to finish, from bottom to top: Sophia bawdy, Sophia ebullient, Sophia sad, Sophia loving, Sophia kittenish, Sophia self-righteous. The actress oozes over the screen and diminishes every other performance except Julien Bertheau's good-natured Napoleon hiding under a veneer of severity and suffering from a recalcitrant family. But there's no reason to doubt Christian-Jacque's wisdom in allow-ing Sophia a free hand, and everybody seems to have enjoyed making this elegant but saucy romp, which if not especially funny is undeniably effervescent. *Madame* is like an enticing fancy macaroon, glorious to the eye and in promise, but it disappears before you've even had a mouthful.'

James R. Silke, *Cinema*: 'Not an art film. Not a bad film. Good for a light evening . . . makes no other attempt than to frolic with an unreal past and Sophia Loren. It succeeds. Sophia Loren explodes beauti-fully into wit, warmth, glamour, beauty, sex and director Christian-Jacque doesn't miss a smile, a pinch or a contour . . . Her large Italian warmth and rotund beauty are so compelling, it makes you wonder whether, if Napoleon had met Sophia early in his career, the corporal would have gone any further than sergeant.'

Boccaccio '70

'The Raffle' sketch

1961

Prize. Sophia Loren as Zoe, up for grabs in a raffle contest every week.

Italo-French. Embassy Pictures via 20th Century-Fox. Concordia/Cineriz/Francinex/Gray Film production. *The Raffle* sketch. *Director:* Vittorio De Sica. *Producers:* Antonio Cervu, Carlo Ponti—*inspired by* The Decameron *by* Boccaccio. *Script:* Cesare Zavattini. *Photography:* Otello Martelli. *Editor:* Adriana Novelli. *Music Adaptation:* Armando Trovajoli. (The two other sketches were: *The Job* with Romy Schneider, written by Suso Cecchi d'Amico and the director Luchino Visconti; *The Temptation of Dr. Antonio* with Anita Ekberg and Peppino De Filippo, written by Ennio Flaiano, Tullio Pinelli and the director Federico Fellini.) Eastmancolor. 150 minutes. [No. 2561]

CAST

Sophia Loren . . . . *Zoe*
Luigi Giuliani . . . . *Gaetano*
Alfio Vita . . . . *Cuspet*

STORY

Zoe is employed at a shooting gallery, part of a travelling fair in the Po Valley area of Northern Italy. Stuck with the additional expenses of a pregnant wife, her brother-in-law boss persuades Zoe to offer herself as the top raffle prize every Saturday night. Tickets sell like hot pizza, the gallery packed out with males eager for a glimpse of what could be theirs. Zoe meets and falls for one of the crowd, Gaetano from a neighbouring town, and begins to doubt accommodating the raffle winner . . . who proves to be the meek and mild sexton of the village. He is besieged with financial offers to sell his ticket, but his aged mother persuades him not to pass up this one chance of a good time. Enraged with jealousy, Gaetano drives off the trailer in which Zoe is vainly attempting to raise some response in the totally inexperienced sexton; the wild driving is a *coup de grâce* for the young man's rival. Zoe buys

El Magnifico. Hiding children behind her and flashing her red blouse about, Loren made a magnificent matador when a bull broke loose in the fairground.

Cuspet, the sexton, off with the raffle money and her promise of silence about his inability to collect. As she prepares to start life anew with the man she loves, Cuspet is carried through the streets, hero of the hour, delighting in the cheers of the men and the cries of 'swine' from the women.

NOTES

Ponti's idea was for three of the world's leading directors to present *The Decameron* as if Boccaccio was alive and well and writing in the '70s. There were four directors at the start: Mario Monicelli's factory love story, *Renzo and Luciana*, the least stellar episode, featuring Marisa Solinas and Germano Gilioli, was cut for time. Even so, De Sica, Fellini and Visconti supplied a lengthy lump between them.

Ian Johnson, in *Films and Filming*, felt both Fellini and Visconti had matured while De Sica had not really moved on from his '50s creations. '*The Raffle* is probably the most consistently entertaining, stylistically it is the least interesting and contains none of the brilliant flashes which distinguish the first two episodes. His short anecdote is reminiscent of the witticisms of *The Gold of Naples* and Loren as the earthy shooting-ring holder whose virtue is raffled regularly to the fairground visitors, returns (with a trace more presence, more ripeness) to the pizza-seller role of *L'Oro*.'

At the time, I considered that 'without Sophia, this would be the weakest episode; with her it's a gay piece of peasant pleasantry, lying somewhere in the Clochemerle region. As Zoe, the shooting-gallery girl, Sophia offers herself every Saturday night to the winner of the raffle. And tickets sell well when most of the prize is revealed—when Sophia, chased by a

Lovers. Sophia with De Sica's choice of new, and jealous, leading man: Luigi Giuliani.

bull, sensibly removes her red blouse . . .'

Felix Barker, *Evening News*: 'Miss Loren's wanton charm mixed with an intangible fastidiousness and sly humour is perfect.'

John Leversey, *Scene*: 'Lightweight stuff. Just at the end, when Sophia Loren decides she will no longer be the prize in a fairground raffle and quietly sends the incompetent winner packing, it has touches of gentleness and feeling.'

Bosley Crowther, *New York Times*: 'The display of Miss Loren's figure is excessive to the point of tedium . . . How Carlo Ponti . . . could have allowed her and Signor De Sica to revert to such artless crudity after their powerful creation of *Two Women* is an incidental mystery.'

Time magazine: 'The fair itself is alive with superb detail, from the smallest of watermelon seeds to the largest of the paunchy Italian farmers with hot breath and sausage fingers. In this *milieu*, Sophia is not a star showing off but a figure that belongs. In an outgrown red dress, her hair a dishevelled beehive, dripping fresh honey, she laughs and smirks and races the blood of the aged. A big bull gets loose and panics the fairground, thundering and charging through the crowds. The animal stops and takes a long fierce look at Sophia. She slowly removes her blouse. The bull stands glazed for a moment, then runs off snorting in inexplicable terror. A man in the crowd speaks for all when he says "God bless her!"'

Cheered by the vast success of the portmanteau movie, Ponti began dreaming of a *Boccaccio '71*. 'Sophia,' he outlined, 'would play in all three episodes. In one she'd be Italian, directed by De Sica, another a French girl, by Tati, and in the third an Englishwoman, directed by . . .' (pause for effect, and the name dropped made a very good effect) 'Charlie Chaplin.'

Prize-winner. Alfio Vita was the meek church sexton who wins Sophia in a raffle—she gives him the takings instead.

Five Miles To Midnight

Le Couteau dans la Plaie

1962

Franco-Italian. United Artists. Filmsonor (Paris)/ Dear Film (Rome) co-production. *Director/Producer:* Anatole Litvak. *Associate Producer:* André Smagghe. *Script:* Peter Viertel, Hugh Wheeler—*from an idea by* André Versini. *Photography:* Henri Alekan. *Editor:* Bert Bates. *Music:* Mikis Theodorakis. *Art Director:* Alexandre Trauner. *Miss Loren's Costumes:* Guy Laroche. *Sound:* Jacques Carrere. 110 minutes (U.K. 103). [No. 2749]

CAST
Sophia Loren . . . . *Lisa Macklin*
Anthony Perkins . . . . *Robert Macklin*
Gig Young . . . . *David Barnes*
Jean-Pierre Aumont . . . . *Alan Stewart*
Yolande Turner . . . . *Barbara Ford*
Tommy Norden . . . . *Johnny*
Mathilde Casdesus . . . . *Concierge*
William Kearns . . . . *Capt. Wade*
Barbara Nicot . . . . *Mrs. Wade*
Louis Falavigna . . . . *Pharmacist*
Yves Brainville . . . . *M. Dompier*
Elina Labourdette . . . . *Mme. Lafont*
with Guy Laroche and Regine as themselves.

STORY
Impasse—in the marriage of Italian Lisa and Robert Macklin, an ill-tempered, immature American in Paris. As she dances the Twist in a night club, he slaps her face and walks out. He leaves next day for a business trip and Lisa says she does not want to see him again. She is with newspaperman Alan Stewart that evening when she learns Robert's plane has crashed with no survivors. Waking from sedation after the funeral, Lisa finds Robert in the flat: dirty, in pain, but alive! He was thrown clear of the crash by a one-in-a-million chance which has planted another in his mind: obtaining the $120,000 insurance he took out at the airport. Once Lisa collects the money, she will be rid of him. She tries to beg advice from Stewart, but he has been replaced by David Barnes. The insurance formalities take for-

Distraught. But then the script had plenty to answer for . . .

Twist. The dances change yet Sophia handles them all with equal aplomb. This exhibition gets her slapped by husband Anthony Perkins, however.

ever, with Robert hiding in the flat and being discovered by a neighbour's boy, Johnny. Lisa's life becomes a tortuous ordeal, at work, at home, faced with a fugitive husband and a growing love for David, who suspects everything. Finally, the nightmare concludes. She gets the cheque and meets Robert. As they drive to the Belgian border, he reveals he never intended giving her up to Barnes or anyone else. If she dares go, Robert will tell the police all and she will be arrested—an accessory to fraud. Lisa realises she must take the desperate step to freedom. Once taken, there is no turning back. Impasse.

NOTES

Litvak had such great hopes. He refused to have Peter Viertel's adaptation of the Versini plot fully scripted until he knew he had the duet he wanted: re-teaming the illicit lovers from *Desire Under the Elms*. 'In casting Sophia and Tony as the desperate incompatibles, I felt close to impersonating so many couples of the present day. Their contrasting personalities, set in the atmosphere of today's cosmopolitan Paris, reminded me so much of the troubled youngsters of our own experience. Sophia is out-

going, serene, cheerful; she plays a girl from a humble home in Naples who is making good in the sophisticated world of the Paris fashion house. Well, Sophia knew poverty in Naples and she is certainly a success in the sophisticated world of international picture-making. Tony has a gentle, boyish spirit . . . beneath it lie the seeds of violence. I tried the gentle young man I directed in *Goodbye Again* with the dangerous quality he revealed in *Psycho*.'
It did not work out that way.
James R. Silke, *Cinema*: 'Upon seeing Sophia and Tony together, one would never suspect they are married, yet Litvak ignores the possibility of having what seems to be brother and sister, or even mother and son, suddenly and unexpectedly congeal in a passionate embrace. What an opportunity for a Hitchcock or an Aldrich! There are many more opportunities and almost all are missed . . . Sophia Loren's animal vitality is not enough to pull this one out of the mire of mediocrity. Badly cast and badly directed, she presents three distinctly different characters . . . a good, kind-hearted wife who has babied her husband until she no longer respects him . . . an erotic adventuress on the make . . . and a weak woman, tortured by her husband until he drives her

143

Tangle. Perkins (above) comes back from the dead and ruins his wife's new life with reporter Gig Young (right).

to insanity. Which one she is, is never made plain. Your attention is divided between sympathy and suspicion.'

Films and Filming: 'Anthony Perkins' last appearance under Litvak's direction, in *Goodbye Again*, had the advantage of a less involved and more emotionally powerful narrative, together with Ingrid Bergman, with whom Perkins was beautifully matched. I never sensed a similar rapport between Perkins and Loren; they seem to be acting in entirely different films. Sophia Loren, ill-at-ease at the beginning, gradually gathers strength, more from her own personal interpretation of Lisa's reactions than from any font of inspiration provided by Litvak. In the final minutes, the sight of Loren going quietly, tragically insane is really moving and the only time when I felt some sympathy for any of the people on the screen.'

Bosley Crowther, *New York Times*: 'Sophia Loren is given very little opportunity to display her acknowledged talent for acting . . . so much as merely walking through the role. Miss Loren does this to perfection. She's the best walker on the screen. The only trouble is that when she walks, even grimly, it confuses the emotional atmosphere. It takes the viewer's mind off her problem. This happens often in the film.'

Last word from Loren—on Perkins. 'He was right for *Desire Under the Elms*—and I think he was right for this one. He just looks too young. But really, Tony is two years older than I am. But he looks always this very young innocent. Well, now he's married, maybe he changes!'

144

The Condemned Of Altona

I Sequestrati di Altona

1962

Italo-French. 20th Century-Fox. Titanus Films (Rome)/S.G.C. Films (Paris) production. *Director:* Vittorio De Sica. *Producer:* Carlo Ponti. *Script:* Abby Mann—*inspired by the play* Les Séquestres d'Altona *by* Jean-Paul Sartre. *Photography:* Roberto Gerardi. *Editors:* Manuel Del Campo, Adriana Novelli. *Music:* Dmitri Shostakovich: Symphony No. 11, Opus 103. *Conductor:* Franco Ferrara. *Art Director:* Ezio Frigerio. *Wardrobe:* Pierluigi Pizzi. *Make-Up:* Nilo Jacopini; *Loren Make-Up:* Giuseppe Annunziata. *Hairstyles:* Carlo Sindici; *Loren Hairstyles:* Ada Palombi. *Sound:* Ennio Sensi. *Assistant Directors:* Luisa Alessandri, Giuseppe Menegatti. 113 minutes. [No. 2776]

CAST

Sophia Loren	*Johanna*
Maximilian Schell	*Franz*
Fredric March	*Gerlach*
Robert Wagner	*Werner*
Françoise Prévost	*Leni*
Alfredo Franchi	*Grounds-Keeper*
Lucia Pelella	*His Wife*
Roberto Massa	*Driver*
Antonia Cianci	*Maid*
Carlo Antonini	*Police Official*
Armando Sifo	*Policeman*
Aldo Pecchioli	*Cook*

Horror. Sophia Loren's 50th movie—alas, nothing to celebrate about.

Brothers. Married to Robert Wagner (above), Sophia finds his Nazi war criminal brother, Maximilian Schell (right), in hiding at the family manse.

STORY

Gerlach, owner of one of the greatest industrial combines in West Germany, summons his son, Werner, and his actress-wife, Johanna, to the family mansion, Altona. Their trepidation increases as Werner refuses the offered control of the family empire, being against his father's kind of power-consolidation. Werner explains how his brother, Franz, would have controlled everything had he not been killed after being cited at the Nuremburg trials for war-crimes. Hearing terrifying sounds at night, Johanna finds Altona's dread secret. Franz is alive, insane, and being cared for by his sister, Leni. She fills him with tales of Germany's degradation and poverty since the war; Johanna gives him the facts and he runs off to nearby Hamburg, seeking the truth. Confronting Werner with Franz's story of Altona being used, with Gerlach's approval, as a concentration camp, she is disturbed at his lying and his now eager contemplation of running his father's power-base. Arrested in town, Franz is returned to Altona and begs Johanna to forgive his crimes before she leaves. He recalls Smolensk and how, rather than torture Russian farmers for information, he led his

147

Stage-y. Sophia played a stage actress; the film was even more theatrical: a collosal let-down.

troops the wrong way and 500 were killed. Johanna takes pity and tries to expiate his guilt. Leni forces the truth out of him: he had tortured and killed not once, but several times. Realising how deep is the guilt he shares with Gerlach, Franz leaps to his death from scaffolding—dragging his father with him. And the dead symbols of a dead Germany are surrounded by the industrial sounds of the new Germany's power and conquest.

NOTES

Everyone came unstuck on this film: Loren, Ponti, De Sica; particularly poor Sartre. Iris Murdoch has called him a romantic rationalist: he needs every ounce of both attributes to recover from this totally misconceived *mélange* of his philosophical tract on guilt; not Franz's alone, nor Germany's, but that of the human race. (Including Abby Mann and De Sica.) Sad, considering this was Loren's 50th film.

Of course, the distributors were at a complete loss, flogging out near-horror movie come-ons like: 'Academy Award stars tell the shocking story of what happened in the mansion called Altona.' Worse still, and much allied to De Sica's belief about distributors having no taste, the British poster featured

Schell lusting at Loren, naked back to camera . . . with the line: 'A recluse sees a woman for the first time in 15 years!'

Critically, Bosley Crowther took it easy and said *Altona* was condemned to the fate of a disappointing film. Tom Milne in the *Monthly Film Bulletin* hit much harder: 'This film is such a hopeless mess that it is difficult to know where to begin criticising it . . .'

Gordon Gow, *Films and Filming*: 'A muddled piece of film-making, lunging erratically from melodrama to neo-realism, it retains the dramatic onslaught of Sartre's play. Essentially, of course, it is a thing of the theatre, too organised and extravagant at any rate to belong in De Sica's kind of cinema. Sophia Loren has the worst of it, because the sister-in-law is a trying character, always taking the clear view in a situation that is clouded, and bestowing and withdrawing compassion too neatly for comfort. Allowing for a part that might well give any actress pause, she manages nobly . . .'

Stanley Kaufman, *The New Republic*: 'Sophia Loren tries earnestly but is miscast as the actress—too melony and modern and without the bitter, slim-flame quality.'

Yesterday, Today And Tomorrow

Ieri, Oggi e Domani

1963

Italian. Embassy Pictures via Paramount. Champion/Concordia production. *Director:* Vittorio De Sica. *Producer:* Carlo Ponti. *Executive Producer:* Joseph E. Levine. *Photography:* Giuseppe Rotunno. *Editor:* Adriana Novelli. *Music/Conductor:* Armando Trovajoli. *Art Director:* Ezio Frigerio. *Décor:* Ezio Altieri. *Costume Designer:* Piero Tosi. *Costumes:* Annamode. *Sound:* Ennio Sensi. *Assistant Director:* Luisa Allesandri. *Anna-Dresses:* Christian Dior. *Anna-Hats:* Jean Barthet. *Mara-Choreography:* Jacques Ruet. Techniscope. Technicolor. 119 minutes. [No. 3054]

Cartoon by Sam Norkin.

CAST

1. *Adelina/Naples*
   Script: Eduardo de Filippo, Isabelle Quanantotti.

Sophia Loren	*Adelina*
Marcello Mastroianni	*Carmine*
Aldo Giuffre	*Pasquale Nardella*
Agostino Salvietti	*Lawyer Verace*
Lino Mattera	*Amedeo Scapace*
Tecla Scarano	*Bianchina Verace*
Silvia Monelli	*Elvira Nardella*
Carlo Croccolo	*Auctioneer*
Pasquale Cennamo	*Police Captain*

2. *Anna/Milan*
   Script: Cesare Zavattini, Billa Billa—*from a story by* Alberto Moravia.

Sophia Loren	*Anna*
Marcello Mastroianni	*Her Lover*
Armando Trovajoli	*The Other Man*

3. *Mara/Rome*
   Script: Cesare Zavattini.

Sophia Loren	*Mara*
Marcello Mastroianni	*Rusconi*
Giovanni Ridolfi	*Umberto*
Tina Pica	*Grandmother*
Gennaro di Gregorio	*Grandfather*

STORIES

1. *Adelina* hides among her Forcella slum neighbours as police arrive to arrest her for selling contraband cigarettes. But Adelina is pregnant and Italian law stipulates that no mother-to-be can be jailed until six months after delivery, to allow sufficient breast-feeding time. To stave off jail, therefore, Adelina coaxes her unemployed husband, Carmine, into one

Sophia as Adelina: pregnant every year to avoid jail until husband Marcello Mastroianni lets her down ('You fairy!') and she screams out her term; but Marcello talks to the Press and all's well that ends swell!

baby after another until the brood numbers seven. She blooms; he swoons. 'You fairy!' she snarls. The strain is too much for him and finally Adelina goes inside, taking her two youngest daughters with her. Carmine rallies support to pay her fine. The Press pick up the story—and the tab. Italy's president commutes her sentence. Carmine gets a job and, after Adelina's welcome-home party, the entire family play special tribute to their most precious ally—the four-poster bed.

2. *Anna*, swishly elegant wife of a rich Milan industrialist, is out with her lover, a struggling writer. She

muses on how he has brought freshness into her existence, providing things never given by her husband, business-addicted, who provides material needs alone. Reluctantly, the lover agrees to take the wheel of her Rolls convertible, and lost in joint day-dreams of carefree adventures together, he almost runs down a small boy. His swerving dents a fender and Anna panics at the damage and blames 'that little so-and-so'. The lover is shocked, thinking the car more valuable to her than a child's life. A rear tyre catches fire and he grabs her discarded mink to smother the flames and Anna is furious—'use your own coat'.

Sophia as Anna: rich, swish Milanese, trysting with writer Mastroianni.

His utter lack of her kind of worldliness and her concern for material possessions grow more apparent . . . until, when a bald man, unattractive but obviously of her *milieu*, drives up in his luxury car, Anna does not hesitate in accepting a lift back to the city —and summarily telling the writer to stand guard over the Rolls until garage-men arrive.

3. *Mara* infatuates a young neighbour in their apartments overlooking the Piazza Navone. Which is surprising as Umberto is a seminary student and Mara, a call-girl—usually heavily occupied with her most passionate admirer, the ever-impatient Rusconi from Bologna. 'I'm a volcano! Do a striptease with just the refrigerator light on!' Their first chance to be alone and do what comes naturally is interrupted by Umberto's granny, accusing Mara of corrupting the lad, then pleading for help as Umberto refuses to believe the truth about Mara and is threatening to quit the seminary. Rusconi, beside himself with frustration, is then interrupted at another crucial moment by the grandmother. Now she tells Mara that the boy is planning to enlist in the Foreign Legion. Mara comes clean with Umberto and reveals the truth about herself; his tears signal his saving. He returns to the seminary and Rusconi returns to the job in hand—but foiled again. Because of Umberto, Mara has made a vow of chastity for a week! Poor Rusconi could do little else but kneel in prayer alongside Mara at her bedside altar and wait

Sophia as Mara: Roman call-girl, enjoying her calling, and her encouragement from Mastroianni's brilliantly played Bologna playboy, a fore-runner of his kinkier rôles in the 70's.

out the next interminable seven days . . .

NOTES

The Class of '55 re-united! De Sica had steered Sophia to her Oscar, Mastroianni had sure-footed his way through the varying heady pitfalls of Antonioni, Visconti and Fellini (twice), and although a director-to-be in Mike Sarne attacked the continuing philistinism of De Sica—'it's as if *The Leopard* had never been made, *8½* was from another world'— the world loved the trio's trio and paid upwards of $8,000,000 to enjoy the film which went on to win the Oscar for Best Foreign Language Film in 1964. The *News of the World* thought Sophia was enough to ignite celluloid, the *Evening News* felt, bravo, here at last was a chance to see her sense of fun, and the

Sunday Mirror's Jack Bentley would not have missed it for ten epics! Gordon Reid, *Continental Film Review*, felt she was good as Adelina, not so good as Anna and superb as Mara, but left main plaudits to Marcello.

Alexander Walker, *Evening Standard*: '. . . isn't quite good enough for me to say, Move Over Boccaccio—but observe the wit and guile that Vittorio De Sica brings to . . . three episodes . . . every one of them is a highly expert exercise in the Brinkmanship of Bad Taste . . . Now the allure of Sophia Loren is placed somewhat higher than the womb and there's an early limit to the fun that can be had from false pregnancies . . . It's made into a victory for motherhood, if not for family planning . . . She dominates it like the star she is, whether

flouncing big-hipped through the market or cattily dragging her Dior coat in the dirt.'

Mike Sarne, *Films and Filming*: 'Our heroine plays her part (Adelina) as a kind of colour version of her role in *Two Women*, a bit jollier, perhaps a little more daringly coy (we have on two occasions Sophia just about to extract a matriarchal breast for a squawling infant, before the editor cuts away—strong stuff!), but it is the same girl, all right. Sophia, out of her depth as a rich playgirl . . . terribly desirable but she is never more than sexy in the part of a call-girl named Mara who teaches a poor ecclesiastical tyro into almost giving up the frock while the hilarious Marcello bites his fingernails in the bedroom.'

Stanley Kaufman, *The New Republic*: 'Miss Loren's Neapolitan is her *Gold of Naples* pizza-seller all over

Sophia as Mara: showing *Gilda* how in a tumultuous strip for client Mastroianni, choreographed by Jacques Ruet, dance-master at the Crazy Horse Saloon in Paris. 'A marvellous pupil,' said he, 'completely un-selfconscious which is the second requirement of the art.' Nobody had to ask about the first … Says Sophia: 'It was fun to make!'

again, hearty, shrewd and in several cases, free-swinging. As the Milanese, she has the appropriate bored *tristesse*. Her Romana is a somewhat sloppy sentimentalist about everything but her job.'

Ironically released in Britain at the same time as Gina Lollobrigida, long since left way behind with her press cuttings on the old rivalry race, also turned in a strip-tease routine in Giancarlo Zagni's *La Bellezza di Ippolita/The Beauty of Ippolita*. She

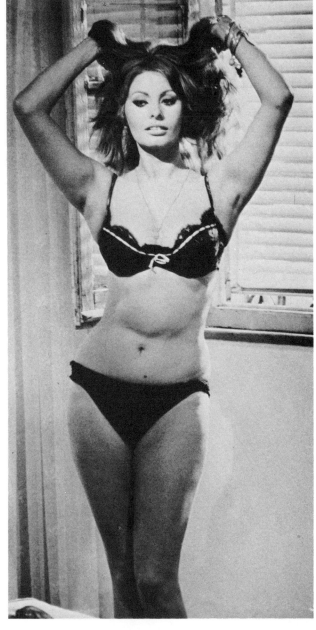

thrashed around as a chorus-stripper in black tights, shiny bra, fringey pants, plumes and feathers—without one-sixth the erotic-fun impact of Sophia's Mara. U.K. release title for La Lollo's effort was perhaps cruelly apt: *She Got What She Asked For*. Lollo certainly did not get rave reviews like this hosanna to Loren's strip from James R. Silke in *Cinema*: 'The scene will intoxicate the male audiences as it does Mastroianni and make women aware of their own physical potential. De Sica creates a fantasy right out of the Twenties, a tantalising, mysterious vamp, the possessor of all female delights, and he just as quickly reverses the situation by having the girl remain celibate for a week in order to help save the young priest for the church. This topic of reversal would be acceptable to an audience only when done by a performer with Sophia's talent for portraying both wanton and virgin.'

In fact about the only thing wrong with this film is the title: all the sketches seemed to take place today, which is yesterday now, but never was tomorrow . . . Ponti's original notion would have been better, if a shade too commercial: *Three Women*.

It's obvious enough on-screen, but Loren adores the De Sica comedies in Naples (and they have not finished making them yet). 'They're fun,' she says. 'They don't enter into the usual routine of a comedy where you always know what is going to happen next. Italian comedies are always quite original, I think. They're still hard to make, sometimes even harder than a fully dramatic piece. We still manage to have fun doing them!'

The Fall Of The Roman Empire

1964

American-Italian. Rank. Samuel Bronston Productions/Roma Film co-production. *Director:* Anthony Mann. *Producer:* Samuel Bronston. *Associate Producers:* Michael Waszynski, Jaime Prades. *Script:* Ben Barzman, Basilio Franchina, Philip Yordan. *Photography:* Robert Krasker. *Editor:* Robert Lawrence. *Music:* Dmitri Tiomkin. *Production Design:* Veniero Colsanti, John Moore. *Special Effects:* Alex Weldon. *Sound:* David Hildyard, Gordon K. McCallum. *Second Unit Team: controller*, Andrew Marton; *director:* Yakima Canutt; *photography:* Cecilio Paniagua. Ultra-Panavision. Technicolor. 187 minutes.

CAST

Sophia Loren	*Lucilla*
Stephen Boyd	*Livius*
James Mason	*Timonides*
Christopher Plummer	*Commodus*
Alec Guinness	*Marcus Aurelius*
Anthony Quayle	*Verulus*
Omar Sharif	*Sohamus*
John Ireland	*Ballomar*
Mel Ferrer	*Cleander*
Eric Porter	*Julianus*
Douglas Wilmer	*Niger*
Peter Damon	*Claudius*
Andrew Keir	*Polybius*
George Murcell	*Victorinus*
Lena von Martens	*Helva*
Gabriella Licudi	*Tauna*
Norman Wooland	*Virgilianus*
Rafael Luis Calvo	*Lentalus*
Virgilio Texera	*Marcellus*
Michael Gwyn	*Cornelius*
Guy Rolfe	*Marius*
Finlay Currie	*Caecina*

Millionairess. Sophia played Lucilla for a reputed million dollars. The sets were not cheap either.

Chained. Loren and Stephen Boyd's Livius about to be burnt at the stake.

Paternal. Sir Alec Guinness as Emperor with Sophia as his daughter.

STORY

Marcus Aurelius Antonius, philosopher-emperor of Rome, summons his empire's governors and princes to German war headquarters for a Pax Romanus. He confides to his daughter, Lucilla, that his adopted son, Livius, will succeed him instead of his more unstable heir, Commodus. Overhearing this, Cleander, a blind prophet loyal to Commodus, presents Marcus with a poisoned apple. After the funeral, Livius, who does not share Lucilla's ambition for himself or Rome, allows Commodus to proclaim himself emperor. Lucilla marries Sohamus of Armenia. While pestilence ravages Rome, Commodus continues his vain, licentious behaviour, neglecting all symptoms of unrest while banishing anyone reminding him of his responsibilities: Livius, Lucilla, Timonides the Greek. Livius remains loyal during an Eastern revolt, and when Sohamus is killed in battle, he takes Lucilla back with him to Rome. Enraged by Livius' refusal to support his tottering throne, Commodus retaliates

by destroying a newly free Barbarian village; Timonides is killed in its defence. During the Saturnalia, Commodus buys Livius' army with gold; slays Verulus, his gladiatorial tutor, on hearing that he and not Marcus was his real father; chains Lucilla to a stake in the arena; and proclaims himself a god. This insane conceit leads him into rash combat with Livius—which he loses. Livius frees Lucilla from the blazing pyre, and while Commodus' senators bid for the vacant throne, Livius and Lucilla turn their back on the corruption of Rome.

NOTES

Crammed full with all the current stellar names—and with the inevitable epic rôle for Finlay Currie, 86; he was in *Quo Vadis* too, and most other epics up to his death as the world's oldest working actor at 90 in 1968—the cast was sumptuous, so were the sets, and much of the film. A poor successor, in terms of power and glory, to *El Cid*, and thus it was

Empire Faces. Two views of Lucilla, the above bearing an uncanny resemblance to Elizabeth Taylor.

fated to be just another road-show, of which the cinema had lately had too many, and out of which the musical was forcing a momentary come-back.

Director Anthony Mann found it all a little more tough going than *El Cid*, too. 'It has a defeatist theme. I was very conscious that I might be stepping into a hole doing this, because I just don't think people are interested in defeat.' He was right.

Loren had misgivings. Not about the size or scope of the movie so much as the news that Sir Alec Guinness was playing her father. 'He was a great surprise to me. When I knew he was going to be in the film I was a bit scared. After all, he has a title

and I thought he would be rather pompous. But he was marvellous; we loved each other. I used to go to his house all the time. We used to do the Twist together. He did it very well!'

Bosley Crowther, *New York Times*: 'Sophia Loren is ornamental, without intelligence or sex, as Commodus' beautiful sister, who for some strange reason loves the general.'

Sight and Sound: '. . . the statuesque presence of Loren reminds one of what Rome can offer in grace and richness.'

Naples, as always, was about to improve on that!

Marriage, Italian Style

Matrimonio all'italiana

1964

Italo-French. Embassy Pictures via Paramount. Champion (Rome)/Les Films Concordia (Paris) co-production. *Director:* Vittorio De Sica. *Producer:* Carlo Ponti. *Executive Producer:* Joseph E. Levine. *Script:* Eduardo de Filippo, Renato Castellani, Antonio Guerra, Leo Benvenuto, Pier de Barnardi— *from the play* Filumena Marturano *by* de Filippo. *Photography:* Roberto Gerardi. *Editor:* Adriana Novelli. *Music:* Armando Trovajoli. *Art Director:* Carlo Egidi. *Costume Designers:* Piero Tosi, Vera Marzot. *Costumes:* Annamode. *Sound:* Ennio Sensi. Eastmancolor. 102 minutes (U.K. 100). [No. 3240]

CAST

Sophia Loren	*Filumena Marturano*
Marcello Mastroianni	*Domenico Soriano*
Aldo Puglisi	*Alfredo*
Tecla Scarano	*Rosalie*
Marilu Tolo	*Diane*
Pia Lindstrom	*Cashier*
Giovanni Ridolfi	*Umberto*
Vito Moriconi	*Riccardo*
Generoso Cortini	*Michele*
Raffaello Rossi Bussola	*Lawyer*
Vincenza di Capua	*Mother*
Vincenzo Alta	*Priest*

STORY

Naples, 1964. Wealthy businessman and dandy Domenico, known as Don Dumi, is admiring his fiancée trying her wedding dress, when he is informed his long-timè mistress, Filumena, has been rushed home, unconscious: a priest has been sent for. Reluctantly, he goes to her recalling how he met her ... cringing in a brothel cupboard during a '43 air-raid. He had comforted her and she willingly responded to the first man in her life. After the war, they met again, made love again; he took her from the brothel, set her up in a flat. While he continued his playboy life, she ran his bar and bakery. She next took over his home with equal slapdash

efficiency despite being treated like a servant by his senile, invalid mother, and having to sleep in the servant's room, gliding into his bed each night.
Now to save the dying Filumena from mortal sin, Dumi consents to marry her on her deathbed. She recovers miraculously and demands conjugal rights; he has been tricked. Furthermore, she announces

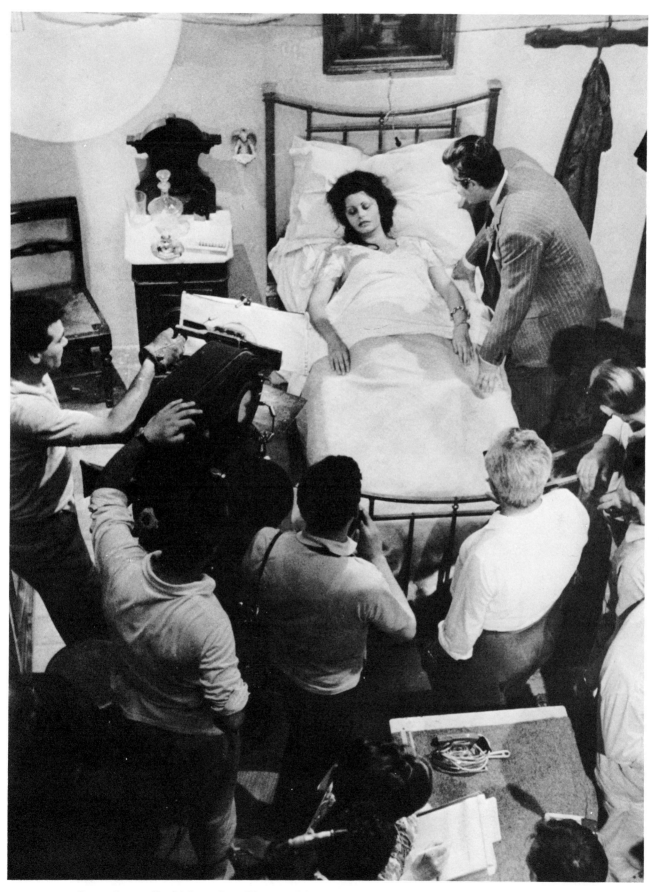

Death Scene. Sophia's so fiery Filumena fakes death-throes to trap Mastroianni into marriage.

three grown sons coming home legally to bear his name. Infuriated, he gets the marriage annulled as a fraud. Filumena then tells him one of the boys is his, but refuses to say which. At first he also refuses to believe her until discovering he could have fathered all three. On Mount Vesuvius, they argue again about the lads and in a struggle, kiss passionately. Irrevocably interwoven, they marry again and all three sons call Dumi, Papa. Filumena, who has never cried in all her life, weeps for joy.

NOTES

Although it was the director's usual compromise between bleak reality and rosier box-office hues, according to Raymond Durgnant—'De Sica's usual attitude of a unique and fainting mixture of Franciscan sentimentality and Marxist hard-headedness'— *Marriage* attained exactly the same kind (and amount) of global financial success as the trio's previous venture. 'Their brightest teaming yet,' said Kevin Keys, *Universe*. 'A very warm, whimsical

Full of Life. The rise and fall and rise again of Eduardo De Filippo's spunky heroine—first found by Marcello Mastroianni as a teenager cowering from war-bombing, next in a bordello, then finally taken into his house and business, running everything while he runs after younger girls—presented Loren with another Oscar-worthy performance with every last stop pulled out. For once, even Mastroianni seemed lost in the avalanche of emotions.

and worldly comedy.'

De Sica hated the title: 'distributors always have bad taste'. Although it would have confused the issue, Ponti's previous idea of *Three Women* would have fitted admirably: '... Loren progresses from brothel ingénue to strutting tart, domineering housekeeper and devoted mother in a way that embraces all womankind,' wrote Alexander Walker, *Evening Standard*.

Raymond Durgnant, *Films and Filming*: 'From the

first shot of Sophia being carried through the streets, ashen-faced, after her suicide, the film has a wistful undertow even in the funniest scenes. She throws some magnificent fits of proud, hard temperament, but also plays with a softness, a sadness that I haven't seen in her playing since *Two Women*. So sumptuous and imperious is Loren, that her sudden flurries of harassed earth-mother never cease to astonish by their warmth and strength.'

Bosley Crowther, *New York Times*: 'Whenever

Vittorio De Sica gets together with Sophia Loren to make a motion picture, something wonderful happens ... a film so frank and free and understanding of a certain kind of woman—and man, too—that it sends you forth from the theatre feeling you've known her—and him—all your life ... Miss Loren is delightfully eccentric, flashy and formidable, yet stiff in her middle-class rigidity and often poignant in her real anxieties.'

James R. Silke, *Cinema*: 'Sophia Loren's figure and movements dominate the grotesque eroticism of a spider-web costume in the bordello scene, the energetic bad taste of a flower-print dress, and the drab make-up and knit sweater of a tired and sick middle-aged woman.'

Although never mentioned in the official publicity, the play had been filmed previously, under its original title, *Filumena Marturano*, produced by Luigi de Laurentiis in 1951, featuring the author, Eduardo de Filippo, and Tamara Lees.

Every poster tells a lie. Joe Levine's Embassy combine could not find *the* scene that summed the film up (for them); so they added Marcello's head to the bus-driver's body ... and made sure the original shot, with Mastroianni looking on, was not distributed too freely.

Every success breeds a satire. Virna Lisi, Loren's latest rival, aped her Mastroianni teamings with George C. Scott in Hollywood's *Not With My Wife, You Don't.*

Operation Crossbow

1965

Anglo-Italian. M.G.M./Carlo Ponti production. *Director:* Michael Anderson. *Producer:* Carlo Ponti. *Script:* Richard Imrie, Derry Quinn, Ray Rigby—*from a story by* Duilio Coletti, Vittoriano Pettrilli. *Photography:* Erwin Hillier. *Editor:* Ernest Walker. *Music:* Ron Goodwin. *Art Director:* Elliott Scott. *Sound:* A. W. Watkins, Gerry Turner. *Special Effects:* Tom Howard. *Assistant Director:* Basil Rayburn. *Production Manager:* Sydney Streeter. Panavision. Metrocolor. 116 minutes.

CAST

George Peppard . . . *Lieut. John Curtis*
Jeremy Kemp . . . . . *Phil Bradley*
Tom Courtenay . . . *Robert Henshaw*
Sophia Loren . . . . . *Nora*
Trevor Howard . . . . *Prof. Lindemann*
John Mills . . . . . . *Gen. Boyd*
Richard Johnson . . . *Duncan Sandys*
Anthony Quayle . . . *Bamford*
Helmut Dantine . . . *Gen. Linz*
Richard Todd . . . . . *Wg. Cdr. Kendall*
Lilli Palmer . . . . . . *Frieda*
Paul Henreid . . . . . *Gen. Ziemann*
Sylvia Syms . . . . . *Constance Babbington-Smith*
Patrick Wymark . . . *Winston Churchill*
Moray Watson . . . . *Col. Kenneth Post*
Richard Wattis . . . . *Charles Sims*
Maurice Denham and Wolf Frees.

NOTES

December 1942. Churchill appoints Duncan Sandys to investigate reports of German trials of a new secret weapon. Aerial photos are searched for anything remotely like a rocket site and destroyed by bombers. The V.1s hit London and the operation steps up. News filters through of more powerful rockets being developed at the Peenemünde range. Three Allied scientist-officers parachute into Holland, posing as Dutch or German staff for the rocket-base. A suicide mission. Henshaw is caught, but reveals nothing before he dies. Curtis has a bad scare when Nora, the wife of the Dutchman he is impersonating, turns up at his hotel. He manages to side-step all obstacles and obtain work with Bradley at Peenemünde. They radio information to London, and at the cost of their lives guide a R.A.F. bombing squadron to the target with lights. The installation is destroyed.

NOTES

An overly star-heavy World War II drama, heading at times into dangerous Errol Flynn-Burma waters; reminiscent, if not so effective, of Vernon Sewell's 1958 British shoe-string budget production, *The Battle of the V.1.*, which featured Milly Vitale—the star of Sophia Loren's first Italian movie, *Cuori sul Mare*, back in 1950.

Tom Courtenay regretted one thing about the production: he never shared a scene with Loren. 'Although it doesn't look that way. In one scene, Peppard says goodbye to me and hello to Sophia, but all three of us were never on-set together. In fact I finished my scenes before she started. Never met her at all.'

Monthly Film Bulletin: 'Even attempts at ruthless realism—the summary shooting of Sophia Loren for instance—turn out to be just another melodramatic convention.'

War. Max Factory style, a million miles from the honest realism of *Two Women*.

Hero(es). Sophia shared her scenes with the heroes George Peppard and Tom Courtenay. Least it looked that way on-screen; on-set, however, Tom (below, left) never even met her.

Lady L

1965

Franco-Italian. M.G.M. Concordia (Paris)/Champion (Rome) production. *Director/Script:* Peter Ustinov—*from the novel by* Romain Gary. *Producer:* Carlo Ponti. *Photography:* Henri Alekan. *Editor:* Roger Dwyre. *Music:* Jean Françaix. *Art Directors:* Jean d'Eaubonne, August Capelier. *Décor:* Maurice Barnathan. *Sound:* William Sivel. Panavision. Eastmancolor. 124 minutes.

CAST

Sophia Loren	*Lady L*
Paul Newman	*Armand*
David Niven	*Lord Lendale*
Claude Dauphin	*Insp. Mercier*
Philippe Noiret (dubbed by Ustinov)	*Gerome*
Michel Piccoli	*LeCœur*
Marcel Dalio	*Sapper*
Cecil Parker	*Sir Percy*
Jean Wiener	*Krajewski*
Daniel Emilfork	*Kobeleff*
Peter Ustinov	*Prince Otto*
Jacques Dufilho	*Beala*
Eugene Deckers	*Koenigstein*
Sacha Pitoeff	*Bomb-Thrower*
Tanya Lopert	*Agneau*
Catherine Allegret	*Pantoufle*
Arthur Howard	*Butler*

Hella Petri, Roger Trapp, Jean Ruppert, Joe Dassin, Jacques Legras, Mario Feliciani, Dorothy Reynolds, Hazel Hughes, Jacques Ciron.

STORY

Lady Lendale, French-born pillar of English aristocracy, arrives home for her 80th birthday celebrations. Time to tell all to her biographer, Sir Percy. She started life as Louise, a laundress in Corsica, joined LeCœur's brothel in Paris and met the love of her life. Not his lordship, but Armand, an idealistic thief, flirting with revolutionaries. She helps him escape police clutches, but in Switzerland he becomes involved anew with Anarchist International's plot to assassinate Bavaria's Prince Otto in Nice. Though penniless and expecting Armand's child, Louise leaves him and, with some money from another of the group, sets up as a widowed countess in a Nice hotel. Here she meets and tries to rob Lord Lendale. He is determined to find a wife, and knowing all about Louise, proposes; she wants Armand safe from the law, and agrees. Lord L whisks them all, Armand and his associates too, off by private train. To Italy, where Armand temporarily recaptures Louise, while pursuing his plots. Tired of Armand's fecklessness, Louise goes to England to become Lady L. Finally she horrifies Sir Percy with startling revelations. She still saw Armand at intervals; all her children, although Lendale by name, are Armand's; she had married him in Switzerland; remained married to both Armand and Lord L. His lordship was quite content with the bigamous arrangement: and Armand, still her husband and lover, has been their chauffeur all these years....

NOTES

The rivalry with La Lollo returns ... Back in Gina Lollobrigida's similarly unhappy Hollywood moment of the '50s, she was slated to be Lady L opposite Tony Curtis as (hopefully) Armand, under Cukor's direction. But then, who was not announced for it at one time or another? And who was not delighted at not making the final, literal L of a trip? Here was, alas, a real bomb (U.S. not U.K. parlance); it hardly ignited, let alone exploded—a mysterious lapse after even a short study of the credits involved in the enterprise. Several cases of mis-casting, of course—Newman's Frenchman much more so than Sophia's English lady; not even Ustinov and Niven pulling double-weight could save the film from itself. Or more important, from its backers. While not in the *Cleopatra* wastage-class, the project had a $2,000,000 price-tag on it long before Ustinov or any of his team arrived on the hoped-for rescue scene.

Apparently, the powers-that-were at Metro—Ponti, too—were so delighted with the film as Ustinov shot it, that they planned a 150-minute roadshow release. Minds were changed as cinema styles

Lovers. Louise (another French laundress) shared her favours with an anarchistic, and terribly mis-cast, Paul Newman—and fine as dandy David Niven.

switched yet again and *Cleopatra* killed the epics, and scenes were whittled and dropped. 'Suddenly,' agrees Ustinov, 'nothing made much sense any more.' He had seen it as a nostalgic picture: 'it did very well in Vienna, which is exactly the kind of town in which I expected it to be successful.' However, no one makes movies just for—or after *A Breath of Scandal*, about—Vienna anymore.

Sophia, though, was rich in her praise of Ustinov: 'The secret of his effectiveness as a director is that he leaves actors free to do what they want to do in a scene. He creates a wonderful atmosphere on the set, one joke after another, and with him it is all spontaneous. He makes me feel like I was relaxing at home with friends rather than working at a studio.'

David Wilson, *Sight and Sound*: 'Sophia Loren makes the best of a difficult rôle and David Niven gives a polished performance as the duke, but Paul Newman is sadly miscast as Armand. Perhaps a mad extravaganza like this is necessarily uneven—or perhaps Ustinov, for all his eccentric brilliance, was the wrong man to direct it. As it is, all one remembers of *Lady L* are its bits and pieces.'

Sophia mainly. Apart from her 80-year-old make-up, she was flawless. Rory Guy, *Cinema*: 'Miss Loren demonstrates her chameleon facility for playing deftly any cinematic style.'

174

(Above) Nostalgia. As Krajewski (Jean Wiener) plays the Chopin etude, memories abound for the fascinating Lady L— the last of Sophia's take-overs from Gina Lollobrigida. (Right) Sophia Loren—octogenarian style.

Judith

1965

American-Israeli. Paramount. Cumulus/Command production. *Director:* Daniel Mann. *Producer:* Kurt Unger. *Associate Producer:* Phil Breen. *Script:* John Michael Hayes—*from a story by* Lawrence Durrell. *Photography:* John Wilcox. *Editor:* Peter Taylor. *Music:* Sol Kaplan. *Production Design:* Wilfred Shingleton. *Art Directors:* Tony Woolard, Tony Rimmington. *Special Art Direction:* Tony Pratt. *Costumes:* Yvonne Blake. *Sound:* David Hildyard. *Special Effects:* Cliff Richardson, Roy Whybrow. *Assistant Directors:* Gerry O'Hara, Yoel Siberg, Ivan Lengyel. *Second Unit Director/Additional Photography:* Nicolas Roeg. Panavision. Technicolor. 109 minutes.

CAST

Sophia Loren . . . . *Judith*
Peter Finch . . . . *Aaron Stein*
Jack Hawkins . . . . *Major Lawton*
Hans Verner . . . . *Gustav Schiller*
Zaharira Charifai . . . . *Dr. Rachel*
Shraga Friedman . . . . *Nathan*
Joseph Gross . . . . *Yaneck*
Zipora Peled . . . . *Hannah*
Terence Alexander . . . . *Carstairs*
Gilad Constantiner . . . . *Dubin*
Alexander Yahalomi . . . . *Zvi*
Frank Wolff . . . . *Eli*
Andre Morrel . . . . *Chaim*
Aldo Foa . . . . *Interrogator*
Roger Beaumont . . . . *Zeer*
Daniel Ocko . . . . *Arab Guide*
Roland Bartrop . . . . *Aba*
Peter Burton . . . . *Conklin*
John Stacey . . . . *Researcher*

STORY

Palestine, 1947. War is imminent as soon as Israel is declared a state and the British withdraw. Haganah underground forces hear that Nazi war criminal Gustav Schiller is training Arab forces and smuggle in his Jewish wife as an illegal immigrant to help identify him. She is willing, not for Israel, but for herself: Schiller denounced Judith and their son to the Nazis in the war; she survived the concentration-camp horror and the son is presumed dead. Haganah leader Aaron Stein cunningly pushes Judith together with Major Lawton, British officer-in-charge, and he shows her Schiller's address in Damascus. The Haganah go hunting. Judith finds Schiller first and shoots him before he can be interrogated. Stein brings the wounded man back to Palestine, but he refuses to talk about the disposition of forces. The British leave: the attack begins. In the confusion, Judith goes to Schiller and threatens his life again. Scared, he reveals all the Arab plans and tells her their son is alive: he will say where if she can guarantee Schiller's life. The advance is repelled; Schiller is killed by a shell. Stein comforts Judith and promises that he will find her son.

NOTES

Israelis are the new Red Indians of the screen. Their image, struggle and bloodshedding history is treated as inanely as the Apaches of the West. As if Preminger's *Exodus* had not been enough in 1960, here was another slice of Israel, Hollywood style—and, Lord help them, they had *Cast a Giant Shadow* to come in '66. The next Israeli war will be in Los Angeles.

As before, Loren looked good in hot-pants, sounded

Hitching. A ride, a strap and her driver's concentration.

Identification. Sophia shows Judith's concentration camp number to Jack Hawkins and Peter Finch.

Assignation. Judith dallies with the British commander, Jack Hawkins, to gain information.

good, and revelled in the sun, but it was a very strange confection to swallow, riddled with inconsistencies as if *Ladies' Home Journal* was covering war fashions. Bosley Crowther, *New York Times*: 'She is lending her name and her presence to a routine cloak-and-dagger film that, without her, would get no more attention—and would deserve no more—than a quickie on the lower end of a double-bill. Even with her and all the cold hostility she brings ... it comes out a disappointing picture, more lurid and loud than lustrous.'

Monthly Film Bulletin: 'After an early sequence in which a huge packing-case is unloaded from a cargo ship and broken open to reveal Sophia Loren, becomingly wan, but as glamorous as ever after a hazardous journey which killed her less fortunate companion, it is a little difficult to take *Judith* very seriously. And nothing that happens subsequently is any less risible, as Sophia Loren prances crossly about the kibbutz in the briefest of shorts as the inhabitants stare at her pop-eyed (as well they might) and Jack Hawkins nobly refuses to take advantage after setting her up in an hotel bedroom for the purpose.'

For Sophia, the film meant another Mann in her life —the third and last. Delbert Mann, ex-Yale and N.B.C., handled her Hollywood début, *Desire Under the Elms*; Anthony Mann, ex-Triangle Theatre, Theatre Guild and Selznick talent scout, helmed both her mighty Bronston epics in Spain; and now Daniel, ex-musician, Neighbourhood Playhouse and Actors' Studio, who had directed Magnani to her Oscar in *The Rose Tattoo*, entered the lists—sadly below par. Incidentally, none of the Manns is related, except in fluctuating talent and occasional selection of the same actors.

Trap. Sophia and Finch set out to trap her ex-Nazi husband in *Judith*.

Arabesque

1966

American. Rank/Universal (U.S.). Stanley Donen Enterprises production. *Director/Producer:* Stanley Donen. *Associate Producer:* Denis Holt. *Script:* Julian Mitchell, Stanley Price, Pierre Martin—*from the novel* The Cipher *by* Gordon Cotler. *Photography:* Christopher Challis. *Editor:* Frederick Wilson. *Music:* Henry Mancini. *Art Director:* Reece Pemberton. *Loren Wardrobe:* Christian Dior. *Sound:* John W. Mitchell, C. Le Mesurier. *Assistant Director:* Eric Rattray. *Production Manager:* David W. Orton. Panavision. Technicolor. 105 minutes.

CAST
Gregory Peck . . . . *David Pollock*
Sophia Loren . . . . *Yasmin Azir*
Alan Badel . . . . *Beshraavi*
Kieron Moore . . . . *Yussef Kassim*
Carl Duering . . . . *Hassan Jena*
John Merivale . . . . *Sloane*
Duncan Lamont . . . . *Webster*
George Coulouris . . . . *Ragheeb*
Ernest Clark . . . . *Beauchamp*
Harold Kasket . . . . *Mohammed Lufti*

Re-tread. Stanley Donen's thriller was heavily into his *Charade* mould; Sophia was excellent but Gregory Peck was no substitute for Cary Grant.

Escape. Loren and Peck and Carl Duering were kept on the run from an ever-increasing number of Arab baddies—everywhere from Ascot races to bone-crushing building-sites.

STORY

David Pollock, American professor at Oxford on an exchange plan, agrees to decipher a hieroglyphical message for oil magnate Nejim Beshraavi—because a Middle-East premier, Hassan Jena, has asked Pollock to spy on Beshraavi in the interests of world peace. Nothing comes easy, though. At the magnate's plush London residence, Pollock is warned by Beshraavi's exotic mistress, Yasmin Azir, that he will be slain once he has completed his translations. Holding a pair of scissors to the girl's throat, Pollock makes his escape but soon falls into the equally oily clutches of Beshraavi's rival, Yussef Kassim, who tries to kill him and the girl with a demolition crane. Amid much more plot and counter-plot, the couple discover the cipher's secret and, with Yasmin's assistance, prevent the assassination of Premier Jena.

NOTES

Charade re-visited—by the same film-maker and firm believer in good old star quality, Stanley Donen. While the teaming of Peck and Loren did not exactly sparkle with the self-same magic as the previous thriller's Cary Grant and Audrey Hepburn, it had its moments in between a similarly confused and finally illogical over-weaved plot, and what one critic referred to as Donen's heartfulness and relish for violent death. And Sophia, minus a final vowel for the second consecutive movie, looked, needless to say, sumptuous when dressed by Dior or a (too) handy bath towel.
Monthly Film Bulletin: 'Everybody seems far fetched

rather than clever; the characters portrayed by Loren and Peck are respectively too brazen and too improbable to be cared about at all ... there is Sophia Loren clambering across a suspension bridge with her skirt neatly slit up to the thigh, or dashing to the rescue in shiny PVC. Nothing could look more "with it", or somehow matter less.'

Grace Glueck, *New York Times*: 'Sophia Loren, a stunning bit of animated scenery, who is not called upon to act but to Dior. She manages to accomplish this seductively both in and out of a series of lavish costumes and through such tribulations as murder, boudoir scenes with a fetishist lover and pursuit in a construction pit by a steel wrecking ball.'

Well dressed. Donen's budget for what he called 'a kind of ornamentation consisting of fantastic interlacing patterns' included a £50,000 clothes bill from Marc Bohan of Dior for Sophia. Including 50 pairs of shoes to delight her fetishistic protector, Alan Badel.

A Countess From Hong Kong

1966

American. Rank/Universal (U.S.). Universal production. *Director/Script/Music:* Charles Chaplin. *Producer:* Jerome Epstein. *Photography:* Arthur Ibbetson. *Editor:* Gordon Hales. *Music Associate:* Eric James. *Arranger/Conductor:* Lambert Williamson. *Art Director:* Bob Cartwright. *Sound:* Bill Daniels, Ken Barker. Technicolor. 120 minutes (U.S. 107).

CAST

Marlon Brando	*Ogden*
Sophia Loren	*Natascha*
Sydney Chaplin	*Harvey*
Tippi Hedren	*Martha*
Patrick Cargill	*Hudson*
Michael Medwin	*John Felix*
Oliver Johnston	*Clark*
John Paul	*Captain*
Angela Scoular	*Society Girl*
Margaret Rutherford	*Miss Gaulswallow*
Peter Bartlett	*Steward*
Bill Nagy	*Crawford*
Dilys Laye	*Saleswoman*
Angela Pringle	*Baroness*
Jenny Bridges	*Countess*
Arthur Gross	*Immigration Officer*
Balbina	*French Maid*
Charles Chaplin	*Old Steward*

Anthony Chin, Jose Sukhum Boonlve, Janine Hill, Burnell Tucker, Leonard Trolley, Len Lowe, Francis Dux, Cecil Cheng, Ronald Rubin, Michael Spice, Ray Marlowe, Kevin Manser, Marianne Stone, Lew Luton, Larry Cross, Bill Edwards, Drew Russell, John Sterland, Paul Carson, Paul Tamarin, Carol Cleveland, Geraldine Chaplin, Josephine Chaplin.

STORY

Natascha, a gorgeous if highly impoverished White Russian countess, stows away on a luxury liner at Hong Kong, determined to seek a new life in America. And does so via a millionaire diplomat, Ogden. She hides in his cabin, causing an endless stream of misunderstandings and complications; particularly when his wife, Martha, joins the trip at Honolulu, necessitating a 'marriage' to Ogden's valet, Hudson, a saronged-dive overboard and more subterfuge on the part of Ogden and his associate, Harvey.

'The story ... resulted from a visit I made to Shanghai in 1931 when I came across a number of titled aristocrats who had escaped the Russian Revolution. They were destitute and without a country, their status was of the lowest grade. The men ran rickshaws and the women worked in ten cent dance halls. When the second World War broke out, many of the old aristocrats had died and the young generation migrated to Hong Kong where their plight was even worse for Hong Kong was overcrowded with refugees. This is the background to *A Countess from Hong Kong*.'—Charles Chaplin.

NOTES

This was the big one of 1966. In publicity terms, the combination of Chaplin's return, coupled with magic chemistry—on paper—of Brando and Loren was front-page and magazine cover-story headline-fodder from Napoli to Ngaruawahia, New Zealand. Alas, once again films being what they are, this was the big let down. 'Although a romance, there is nothing old-fashioned about it,' Chaplin bravely wrote in the royal world premiere programme in January '67. Few critics agreed. The entire project was crucified. 'They don't worry me,' said the 77-year-old, ever brave about his 81st film, the first since 1957's *The King in New York*. 'It's still a great film.' Not even on TV, Charlie ...

Carlo Ponti's germ of an idea, coupled with the rumours the Pontis had heard for some years about Chaplin writing something specifically with Sophia in mind, first became tangible when Sophia met the old master at Vevey while shooting *Lady L* in Switzerland. He mimed his script over dinner, and in recalling their poverty-stricken youth, they struck up the makings of a rewarding relationship. By the time

Goodwill. From when Chaplin announced the project with her at a Savoy Hotel reception on November 1, 1965, cameras popped and the world's Press wished them well. Fourteen months later, despite Loren, despite Chaplin—*and* a royal world premiere on January 5, 1967—the critical groan was audible the world over. Sophia insists it was a graceful, charming film.

Charles Chaplin

Presents

The story of "A Countess From Hong Kong" resulted from a visit I made to Shanghai in 1931 where I came across a number of titled aristocrats who had escaped the Russian Revolution. They were destitute and without a country, their status was of the lowest grade. The men ran rickshaws and the women worked in ten cent dance halls.

When the second World War broke out many of the old aristocrats had died and the young generation migrated to Hong Kong where their plight was even worse for Hong Kong was overcrowded with refugees.

This is the background to "A Countess From Hong Kong".

I have tried to achieve a simplicity of direction which should lend realism to the situation, and which should create a compelling belief in the comedy.

Although a romance there is nothing old-fashioned about it. Romanticism is as up to date as sex, love or psychoanalysis, and is the "sine qua non" of all humanity . . . life would be a very drab existence without it. Of course I am a romantic, I believe it is as indispensable as life itself. It is the reason we go to the theatre . . . not to solve a problem but to indulge in one. I hope I will achieve your indulgence.

Charles Chaplin

Dance. Loren shows Brando a waltz is no tango.

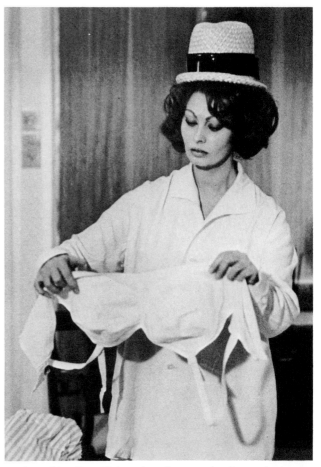

Gag. Chaplin still found undies—and toilets—funny.

shooting began at Pinewood in February 1966, some-one had put the fire out. 'The first day I was scared to death,' recalls Sophia. 'Then I saw Charlie was so nervous, so vulnerable himself, it was like it was going to be his first film. I thought, "My God, I'm not the only one," and felt better right away.'

The publicity department had to keep the hordes away. Few if any, other than Chaplin-approved V.I.P.s (James Baldwin, Patricia Neal included), were allowed on the hallowed set, and when collared into saying anything for posterity, both stars kept up a continual genuflection to Chaplin, despite his con-tinual miming of each character's every move, which had Brando calling himself a glorified marionette. Sophia made a lot of sense when she asked: 'How could you argue with Charlie Chaplin? He started the comedies and if he tells you something, you do it.' (He even showed her how to kiss!) Brando hit the main flaw right in the mouth. 'Charlie's not a verbal man. Words, at times, are his bitterest enemies.'

The film, which probably had more good will and hope going for it than any other in years, tragically underlined this salient fact. Once again, Sophia sur-vived brilliantly in all the circumstances. Alexander Walker, *Evening Standard*: '. . . a sad and bitter disappointment . . . a dialogue comedy written and directed by a man who has always been at his most brilliant when he doesn't depend on words. Here they let him down in scene after scene . . . Miss Loren mostly stays a beautiful mask.'

Bosley Crowther, *New York Times*: 'So the dismal truth is it is awful . . . a numbingly archaic farce.'

Penelope Gilliatt, *Observer*: 'Sometimes this dis-tressingly heavy film is funny . . . Sophia Loren, her sea-lion hips slithering around mesmerisingly in a man's silk dressing gown . . . has a new comedic style, small-gestured and swift, with a sumptuous long stride in low-heeled slippers that is like an oiled version of Groucho's. But the jokes about the size of her bra are fairly ponderous . . .'

Monthly Film Bulletin: 'The saddest thing about this wan romantic comedy, with which Chaplin breaks a ten-year silence . . . is that there is abso-lutely nothing to say about it. The direction is long-winded in the extreme and almost everything about the film is long-winded . . . Sophia Loren plays up nobly.'

Eclipse. Stultified by Chaplin's puppetry direction, Marlon Brando found himself in the unique position of being utterly upstaged by Sophia at her captivating best.

Axel Madsen, *Cinema*: '. . . 107 minutes of senile infantilism by the one man we traditionally call the motion-pictures' greatest comedian . . . Miss Loren is brave because neither hairdressing nor photography is flattering. She comes across as a provincial stock company actress fast approaching menopause and permanent lay-off. If there were such a thing as an Oscar for the most courageous performance by an actress, Miss Loren would be the first-ballot winner.'

Notwithstanding the critics, the film remains a most cherished episode in Loren's career. 'I don't think the

Tussle. And Loren won! Her performance, as Brando had said ten years before about her beauty, was 'the damnedest thing, when you see it you don't believe it. Then you look again ... and still you don't believe it.'

Charles Chaplin
Presents
Marlon Brando & Sophia Loren
"A Countess From Hong Kong"
also starring
Sydney Chaplin & Tippi Hedren
with
Patrick Cargill & Margaret Rutherford
Written, Directed and Music by Charles Chaplin
Produced by Jerome Epstein   Universal Pictures Limited   Technicolor*

film's reception was fair at all. Not for a picture like that, especially one directed by Charlie Chaplin. He is not just anyone; he is someone, Charlie Chaplin. He has invented our profession, our business really; he is one of the pillars with Walt Disney, I think. 'If critics are constructive, I read them even if they are negative to me. If they are destructive, I really get mad! Even if a picture is no good, they have to remember this film represents three months of your life, spending all your energies, having a lot of problems and really working hard. You cannot—or should not—destroy somebody else's work with some clever phrase. This I resent. When they showed *Countess* on television in Italy recently, it got wonderful reviews and deserved them, for it is a graceful film, charming. I would be very pleased if it came out again and they would rediscover it.'

Protective. Sophia retains blissful memories of the film, and has high hopes it will be re-discovered. 'It had all the grace that only Charlie Chaplin could have put in it ...'

Cinderella, Italian Style

C'era una Volta
a.k.a. Happily Ever After
(More Than a Miracle [U.S.])

1967

Italo-French. M.G.M. Champion (Rome)/Les Films Concordia (Paris) co-production. *Director:* Francesco Rosi. *Producer:* Carlo Ponti. *Script:* Tonino Guerra, Raffaele La Capria, Giuseppe Patroni Griffi, Francesco Rosi. *Photography:* Pasquale De Santis. *Editor:* Jolanda Benvenuti. *Music:* Piero Piccioni. *Art Director:* Piero Poletto. *Costumes:* Giulio Coltellacci. *Sound:* Claudio Marcelli, Mario Morigi. *U.S. Title Song:* Larry Kusik, Eddie Snyder; *sung by* Roger Williams. Franscope. Technicolor. 103 minutes. [No. 3812]

CAST

Sophia Loren . . . . . . *Isabella*
Omar Sharif . . . . . *Prince Ramon*
Dolores Del Rio . . . . *Queen Mother*
Georges Wilson . . . . *Monzu*
Leslie French . . . . . *Brother Joseph de Copertino*
Marina Malfatti . . . . *Devout Princess*
Anna Nogara . . . . . . *Impatient Princess*
Rita Forzano . . . . . . *Greedy Princess*
Rosemary Martin . . . *Vain Princess*
Carlotta Barilli . . . . . *Superstitious Princess*
Fleur Mombelli . . . . *Haughty Princess*
Anne Liotti . . . . *Infant Princess*
Carla Pisacane, Gladys Dawson } *Witches*
Kathleen St. John, Beatrice Greack }
Chris Herta, Pietro Carloni, Giovanni Tarallo, Renato Pinciroli, Giacomo Furia, Pasquale Di Napoli, Francesco Coppola, Salvatore Ruro, Vincenzo Danaro, Luciano Di Mauro, Luigi Criscuolo, Francesco Lo Como, Valentino Macchi.

STORY

Naples, *circa* 1600. Once upon a time Spanish Prince Ramon was too fond of the sporting life to heed his king's orders that he needs must wed. The prince

194

preferred to find his own twin-soul in his own time. Unseated during a spirited ride, Ramon encounters Brother Joseph, a serene monk with the astonishing power of levitational flight. The monk makes a gift to Ramon of his donkey and a little flour—make seven dumplings from that, eat them all, and Ramon will be ready to choose the right wife. Ramon meets, and flirts, with peasant girl Isabella. She fails the dumpling test (too hungry herself) but anxious to know the prince's true feelings she seeks the aid of a witches' coven. They mistakenly paralyse Ramon with a spell and, upon release, he has Isabella locked in a barrel for punishment as a witch. He then returns home for a special banquet at which he must choose a bride from seven princesses. Hearing that Isabella has followed him and is working in the royal kitchens, Ramon makes her take part in the competition for the would-be royal brides. She loses again and feels so humiliated, she runs off to throw herself into Vesuvius. Brother Joseph—now an angel—flies to her rescue, sends her back and reveals how she was cheated in the contest. Ramon takes her for his bride and, of course, they live happily ever after.

NOTES

A complete departure from any of the several proven Loren vehicles—and a hint of the personal happiness in store. Sophia and Carlo had agreed on a semi-retirement in order, this time, to make sure of keep-ing her baby and giving birth. And so to help put her in the maternal mood, a fairy story for her children to come . . . Starting off, appropriately enough, as *Once Upon a Time*, the finished feature went through all manner of title-switches until—and why not?—they selected the obvious. What else could one call a fairy story from a living fairy story?

Among the most clichéd in any, if not all, of the Loren reviews still available for inspection, is the line about never looking better/more glamorous/so beautiful/lovelier/etc. This time, more than in any other movies, it was glisteningly true. Whether on-screen, stunningly shot by Pasquale De Santis, or in the Tazio Secciaroli stills, the impeccably buoyant Loren features had, indeed, never been more radiant. So much so, Vincent Canby, *New York Times*, called her a one-woman anti-poverty programme:

'It seems that one of Miss Loren's most important functions in her private life is to upgrade those motion pictures produced by her husband, Carlo Ponti, that turn into poverty (not disaster) areas . . . If anyone could save the film of course, it would be Sophia, but even she fails, though she does spend most of the picture in one of those break-away peasant mini-dresses in which she first burst upon the public consciousness. During one sequence, Sophia is entirely hidden in a barrel, which is just another example of how Mr. Ponti has squandered his natural resources.'

Fairy Tale. Once upon a time, there was a beautiful Italian peasant girl who caught the eye of a rich prince-of-all-he-surveyed—she caught a few dishes too—and overcoming various vicissitudes she married him and lived happily ever after. A fairy tale?

Ghosts, Italian Style

Questi Fantasmi

a.k.a. Three Ghosts

1967

Italo-French. M.G.M. Champion (Rome)/Les Films Corona (Paris) co-production. *Director:* Renato Castellani. *Producer:* Carlo Ponti. *Associate Producer/English Dialogue:* Ernest Pintoff. *Script:* Renato Castellani, Adriano Barracco, Leo Benvenuti, Piero De Bernardi—*from the play* Questi Fantasmi *by* Eduardo De Filippo. *Photography:* Tonino Delli Colli. *Editor:* Jolande Benvenuti. *Music:* Luis Enriquez Bacalov. *Art Director:* Piero Poletto. *Sound:* Carlo Palmieri. *Assistant Director:* Maria Teresa Girosi. Technicolor. 120 minutes (U.K. 93). [No. 4023]

CAST

Sophia Loren . . . . *Maria*
Vittorio Gassman . . . . *Pasquale*
Mario Adorf . . . . *Alfredo*
Margaret Lee . . . . *Sayonara*
Aldo Giuffre . . . . *Raffaele*
Francesco Tensi . . . . *Prof. Santanna*
And Marcello Mastroianni as a guest-ghost.

STORY

Naples, 1967. Maria is a local hot-blood fed up with the poverty, marital and financial, caused by her ne'er-do-work husband, Pasquale. When their suicide pact fails, she decides to start afresh with Alfredo. He has lusted after her since she was a kid making fake religious artifacts in his exploited orphanage. He is also the reason Pasquale loses every job he gets. In a renewed plot to possess Maria, Alfredo has the couple made rent-free tenants of a haunted palace. They move in and, unknown to them, Alfredo takes the room above. Pasquale lets another room to prostitute Sayonara and she stands in for Maria on the night she promises to enter Alfredo's bed. Pasquale glimpses Alfredo and takes him for the ghost—but takes the money he drops. Maria thinks her husband is procuring for her—and disappears. Pasquale is charged with murder and tossed in jail. Alfredo keeps a permanent flame lit in Maria's memory in the subterranean cistern beneath the palace. Pasquale is released owing to insufficient evidence after seven

Sophia with Vittorio Gassman.

Ne'er-do-well. Vittorio Gassman as Loren's shiftless husband—their first movie together for 16 years.

Ne'er-do-better. German star Mario Adorf chases Sophia and sees ghosts.

months, and returns home to find Maria alive and well and in hiding. As they contemplate a better future together, Alfredo sees Maria and takes her for a ghost, falls to his knees and wishes to atone for his past sins. Maria suggests contributing all his ill-gotten gains to a charity in her memory—and marriage to Sayonara. Proceeds in hand, Maria and Pasquale move to Scotland as domestics for an eccentric lord in a haunted castle. This time, the *fantasmi* are for real!

NOTES

Not the best picture to rest one's laurels on . . . but once finished, Sophia Loren was missing from the screen for two (for her) most important years. By her return she had achieved the major ambition of her life: motherhood.

Although in many respects a return to the pre-Hollywood Loren projects, *Ghosts* proved to be one of those Italian comedies that gained little in travelling. It was Loren's first screen meeting with Gassman since 1952, and he was no match either for her usual stable and bed mate Mastroianni. (Marcello, in fact, turned up for the final gag, as the headless ghost in a Scottish castle; something of a replay from his *Fantasmi a Roma*, with Gassman and Belinda Lee in 1961.)

201

Fantasmi. Sophia play-acts a ghost and gives Adorf his come-uppance.

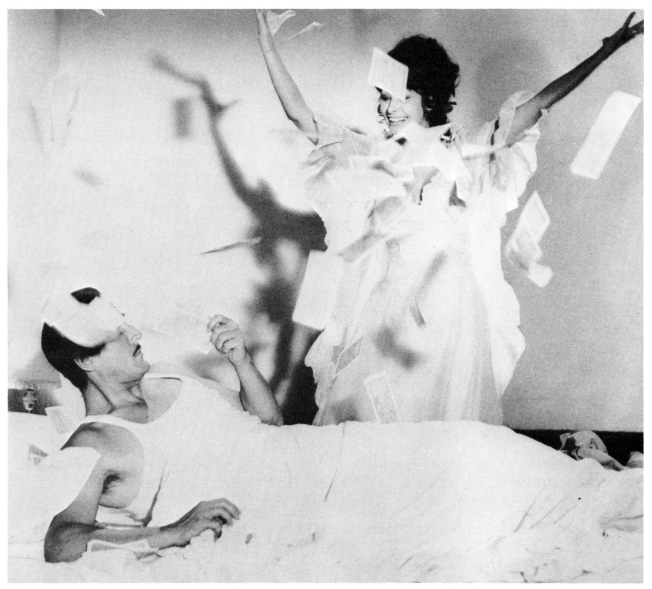

Loot. With Adorf's ill-gotten gains, the couple leave for Britain ...

More ironic was Mario Adorf as Sophia/Maria's would-be lover. Once dubbed the West German Brando, the powerful Adorf has lately become a bigger name in Italian circles and among his '70s rôles was that of Fascist-dictator Benito Mussolini, and the father, of course, of Sophia Loren's brother-in-law.

John Mahoney, *The Hollywood Reporter*: 'To add to the problems inherent in an Italian domestic comedy, a staginess of locations or camera set-ups severely afflicts even a vehicle fortunate enough to have Miss Loren pulling for it . . . Miss Loren plays, scene by scene, ably but differently, too often as if she were taking it all seriously while Gassman reaches for farce, and Adorf seeks to emulate Franco and Cicchio [Italy's Abbott and Costello] in one.'

Next time out, La Loren's co-stars would include . . . Carlo Ponti Jr.

Sunflower

I Girasoli

1969

Italo-French. Avco Embassy. Champion (Rome)/Les Films Concordia (Paris) co-production. *Director:* Vittorio De Sica. *Producers:* Carlo Ponti, Arthur Cohn. *Executive Producer:* Joseph E. Levine. *Script:* Antonio Guerra, Cesare Zavattini, Gheorghij Mdivani. *Photography:* Giuseppe Rotunno. *Editor:* Adriana Novelli. *Music:* Henry Mancini. *Art Director:* Piero Poletto. *Location Art Director:* David Vinitskj. *Costumes:* Enrico Sabbatini. *Sound:* Carlo Palmieri, Alvaro Orsini. *Assistant Directors:* Luigia Alessandri, Paolo Serbandini. *Russian locations* with collaboration of Mosfilm, Moscow. Technicolor. 107 minutes. [No. 4548]

CAST

Sophia Loren	*Giovanna*
Marcello Mastroianni	*Antonio*
Ludmila Savelyeva	*Mascia*
Galina Andreeva	*Soviet Official*
Anna Carena	*Antonio's Mother*
Germano Longo	*Ettore*
Nadia Cerednichenko	*Woman in Sunflower Field*
Glauco Onorato	*Returning Soldier*
Silvana Tranquilli	*Russo-Italian Worker*
Marisa Traversi	*Prostitute*
Guna Zilinski	*Russian Ministry Official*
Carlo Ponti Jr.	*Giovanna's Baby*

STORY

Happiness is short-lived for newly-weds Antonio and Giovanna as the war erupts in Italy. Their 'insanity' plot to release him from the army is discovered and Antonio has the option: jail or volunteer for the Russian front. In action, the freezing cold and starvation rations decimate his comrades and he is only saved from death by peasant girl Mascia. They marry and have a daughter. Years pass and Giovanna's worry turns to resigned grief. Yet—is he really dead? Official ambiguity and apathy provide no clue and she goes to Russia searching military cemeteries, checking names, showing Antonio's snapshot to all she meets. In the Ukraine, she walks through endless fields of sunflowers, symbolising the hopes within her. Finally, her pilgrimage leads to Mascia, her daughter and a short, shattering sight of Antonio. She flees, bitterly, to Italy and lives with a fellow factory-worker, Ettore, older, but much in love with her; they have a son. Restless in Russia, Antonio

With Marcello Mastroianni.

New Fields. Sophia comes back—with Russian locations in the Ukraine.

Old Team. She was safe in De Sica's hands but the screen had grown up and left them far behind.

Co-star. Mastroianni—who else?—played the husband who had to leave her for the war.

wins permission to visit home. He meets Giovanna and they try to recapture their love. Time has moved on apace and her son's cry from the next room shatters mood and illusions. He returns to his Russian life. The affair is over.

NOTES

In her maternity absence, 525 films had been made in Italy. What a comeback this would have been if someone in her circle had been going to the pictures, and seen what was going on! The trouble was, yet again, what looked great on paper in the Ponti files —a modern Odyssey, said De Sica, and the first Italian film, one of the first Western productions ever, to be made inside the Soviet Union—just was not on any more. It did not fit the screen's new format, which, not to be coy about it, meant sex. And sex for real, wherever possible.

Between them, James Bond and *Blow Up* (via Ponti out of Antonioni) had shattered the world of films. Andy Warhol had put away his soup-cans and

Search. Sophia combs the crowds at a football stadium.

Confrontation. Sophia finds her missing husband's new wife, Ludmila Savelyeva.

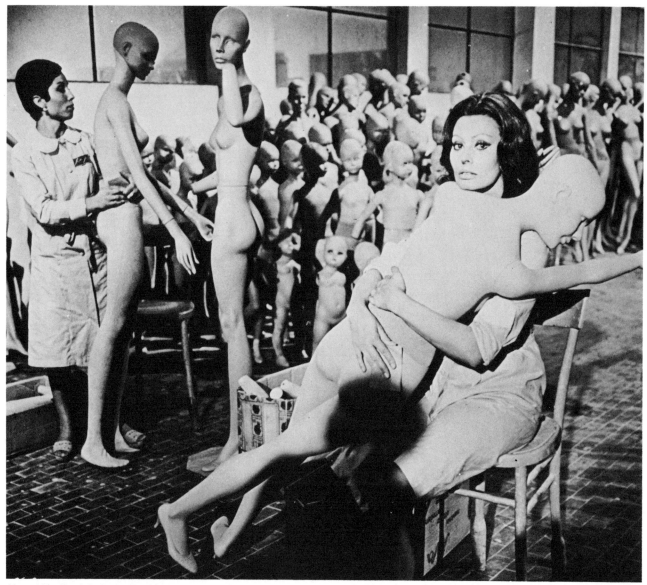

New Life. Back in Italy, Sophia starts life anew without a husband—with fresh career and (right) new man: Germano Longo.

turned his camera on whatever turned-on in front of it. *I'm Curious* said chunky Swede Lena Nyman and the whole world seemed to agree. Everyone was suddenly into films from La Mama Troupe to Norman Mailer. *Easy Rider* had happened and with it, or so Hollywood thought, easy pickings. Coyness was out, eroticism was dropped—except by the masters. Nudity, full-frontal and dorsal, was very much in. Mike Sarne, a severe critic of De Sica, had made *Myra Breckinridge* and seen it earn more than *Yesterday, Today and Tomorrow*. Russ Meyer had been Hollywood bankrolled to shoot *Beyond the Valley of the Dolls* like a Playboy centre-folding orgy. Sam Peckinpah was stirring his calf liver's blood sachets, a young Italian called Bertolucci was being hailed as a genius and dreaming of Marlon Brando and films were being called *The Baby Maker, Sex*

Perverse, Pornography in Denmark, Psychologie des Orgasmus, The Sensually Liberated Female, The Virgin and the Gypsy, and *69*—and meant it!

Not much chance then for a romantic tragedy, Russian locations or not. Conceived as something of a feminine *Doctor Zhivago, Sunflower* could have been made in Yugoslavia, but Ponti, already airing his *Anna Karenina* deal in Moscow, said Russia or not at all. And the wide location sweeps from Moscow to Poltava, in the heart of the sunflower-filled Ukraine, had to be better for Loren and Mastroianni than their love-scenes on the Tor Caldara beach in Italy—which abounded in evil-smelling sulphur deposits.

If motherhood placed an extra bloom to the familiar Loren visage, it did not have much opportunity to shine. For most of the movie, her auburn hair was

streaked with grey and her odyssey clothes were drab indeed. La Ciociara goes East! She went far enough to win the David of Donatello statuette as Italy's best actress of the year for her sorrow-stained performance as the war-abandoned Neapolitan seamstress.

Her reception by Russian crowds was described as tumultuous. 'They ask you for an autograph, and give you fruit, flowers, or something in exchange. They feel that if you give them something, they must give something in return. It's a lovely idea. They reminded me of Neapolitans. There is something very

open about them. They wear their friendliness where you can see it—on their faces.'

A good slice of the publicity went in for the bigamy aspect of the film; De Sica put it down. 'Moral issues are always blurred by war,' said the patriarch and director. 'Personal permutations are always endless.' The role of Mastroianni's second wife was played by Ludmila Savalyeva, best revered for her Natasha in Sergei Bondarchuk's film of *War and Peace*. That was a definitive epic; *Sunflower* was not. 'But,' says Sophia, 'it made a lot of money.'

Time magazine tore the movie to shreds via critic Stefan Kanfer's own mock scenario subtitled 'a fiasco in three acts'. He hurled into the ex-*Time* cover star's work as Giovanna as being a woman of exuberant breasts, thighs of a Gaston Lachaise statue and eyes of a Modigliani portrait—'perhaps that is why no one listens to her voice'.

Kanfer then attempted to bring the Pontis and De Sica up to date with the '70s cinema. 'Why should so many proved talents squander themselves on *Sunflower*? For *pane*? Certainly—but also to counter the sexual revolution with the kind of romantic movie they don't make any more. *Che mal fortuna*—the pornography of sex cannot be replaced by the opera of soap.'

Reunion. Mastroianni returns home and tries to rekindle his love with Sophia. Her baby cries in the next room—it's too late ... time has beaten them. (And their film.)

210

Location: Moscow. De Sica (right) puts Loren through her paces in Russian crowds.

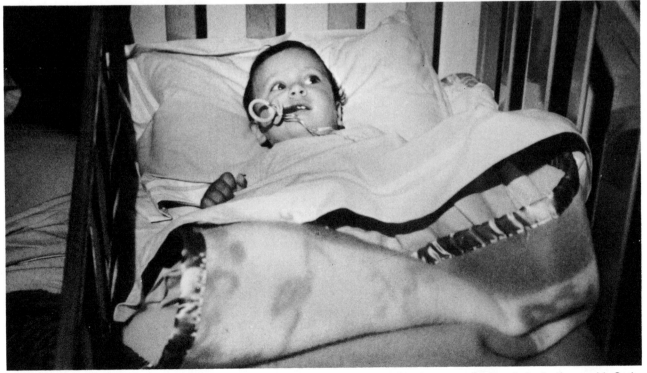

VIP. Missing from the U.S.S.R. locations—but not from the film—was the then most famous baby in the world: Carlo Ponti Jr., known as Chippy from his initials CPJ. Less than a year old, Chippy made a gurgling screen debut in the rôle he knew best. His mother's son.

The Priest's Wife

La Moglie del Prete

1970

Italo-French. Warner Brothers. Champion (Rome)/ P.E.C.F. (Paris) co-production. *Director:* Dino Risi. *Producer:* Carlo Ponti. *Executive Producers:* Pio Angeletti, Andriano De Micheli. *Script:* Ruggero Maccari, Bernardino Zapponi—*from a story by* Maccari, Risi and Zapponi. *Photography:* Alfio Contini. *Editor:* Alberto Gallitti. *Music:* Armando Trovajoli. *Art Director/Costumes:* Gianni Polidori. *Loren Costumes:* Mayer of Rome. *Loren Hairstyles:* Jean Barthet, Paris. *Make-Up:* Guiseppe Annunziata, Guiseppe Banchelli. *Sound:* Claudio Risi. Technicolor. 103 minutes. [No. 4731]

CAST

Sophia Loren . . . . *Valeria Billi*
Marcello Mastroianni . . . . . . *Don Mario*
Venantino Venantini . . . . . *Maurizio*
Jacques Stany . . . . *Jimmy Guitar*
Pippo Starnazza . . . . *Signor Billi*
Augusto Mastrantoni . . . . . . *Monsignor Caldana*
Giuseppe Maffioli . . . . *Davide Libretti*
Miranda Campa . . . . *Signora Billi*
Gino Cavalieri . . . . *Don Filippo*
Gino Lazzari . . . . *Secretary*
Dana Ghia . . . . *Lucia*
Vittorio Crispo, Nerina Montagnana.

STORY

Beautiful but too tall and soft-hearted, Valeria considers suicide after learning that her lover is married; four years and all those gifts down the drain. Re-

Warner Bros. presents a Carlo Ponti production

Sophia Loren   Marcello Mastroianni

TECHNICOLOR*

Warner Bros. **WB** Distributors Ltd.

A KINNEY COMPANY

THE PRIEST'S WIFE

Pop Star. Boosted into headlines by her clerical affair, Sophia makes the charts—billed as The Priest's Wife.

morse and her S.O.S. to a humanitarian organisation save her at the brink. The voice that dissuaded her on the phone materialises alongside her hospital bed: Don Mario. Despite, or because of, the fact that he is a priest, Valeria falls for him. Madly. The cleric, though, is dedicated to his vocation and refuses to compromise conscience or career, until she chases

him from Padua to Torrescura. Their first kiss. His first . . . ever. Don Mario is a man for all that and despite, or because of, her mini skirts and frank exposé of her wild rock-singing past, he feels closer, still more closer. With desire in his blood, he better understands the Church's military treatment of its clergy: massive doses of organised gym, noodles to

numb the senses, male chaperons—and advice from priests to give in to temptation and enjoy a clandestine affair, else resign or, maybe, get castrated. At night he dreams of exploring her body; by day, back in Padua, he passes her off as his sister and writes for a dispensation in order to marry. He meets her parents and visits an old friend who gave up the clergy to wed, only to find him hiding from both his failure and a shrewish wife, in drink. Dispensations take forever. Valeria receives offers to sing as The Priest's Wife and becomes pregnant. A letter from Rome fills them with happiness—but it is merely a promotional invitation to Mario to continue studies in the Vatican. It is the longed-for goal of any poor, provincial priest and he is happy there. Enough to make Valeria realise he is wed already, to the Church.

NOTES

From Moscow to the Vatican—and Loren gets bang up to date. So much so that *The Priest's Wife* was almost beaten to the starting-gate by *The Married Priest* featuring Rossana Podesta and Lando Buzzanca in more carnal variations of the Sophia-Marcello rôles. With De Sica away, similarly turned-on to freshness (by Bresson's Dominique

Fiery. Chased by reporters, Sophia Loren gives a lesson in the gesticulatory art of saying—no!

216

Sanda discovery in *The Gardens of the Finzi-Continis*), Dino Risi returned to a Loren vehicle for the first time since *Scandal in Sorrento*, 15 years before. While the writers pulled her leg about her height in a script for the first time, Sophia looked incongruously chic, by Mayer of Rome, for any cold-water flat inhabitant of Padua, especially one considering herself difficult to marry because of height and poverty. It explained why Mastroianni split his cassock for her, all the same.

Hank Werba, *Variety*: 'In designing *The Priest's Wife* as a family entry, producer Carlo Ponti is trapped by a story that convinces only on an adult level. Sophia Loren in the role of Valeria is a banal dame from Padua who could not possibly penetrate the cloth and heart of passive Don Mario, other than on a physical level. Without carnal situations, the relationship never reaches beyond Miss Loren's aggressive pursuit and Mastroianni's resignation to it. The two principals play the characters for all they are worth but they never seem to get at each other . . . until the switch finale wherein Mastroianni is promoted and, acting on higher ecclesiastical counsel, suggests to his now impregnated fiancée (a secret she guards for the audience) she become his mistress instead of his wife.'

Lady Liberty

La Mortadella

1971

Italo-French. Warner Brothers; United Artists (U.S.). Champion (Rome)/Les Films Concordia (Paris) production. *Director:* Mario Monicelli. *Producer:* Carlo Ponti. *Script:* Suso Cecchi d'Amico, Mario Monicelli, Ring Lardner Jr. *Photography:* Alfio Contini. *Editor:* Ruggiero Mastroianni, *Art Director:* Mario Garbuglia. Eastmancolor. 103 minutes. [No. 5026]

CAST

Sophia Loren	*Maddalena*
Luigi Proietti	*Michele*
William Devane	*Jock Fenner*
Beeson Carroll	*Dominie*

STORY

Flushed with approaching nuptials, Maddalena flies into New York from Italy to wed her fiancé. She has a very special wedding present: a huge, silver-wrapped mortadella baloney sausage. Michele is delighted; the Food and Drug Administration people are not. Maddalena can enter the United States; the sausage cannot. She refuses to give it up: 'It's the principle!' Newspaperman Jock Fenner hears the row and it is played up big in the headlines, but by the time Italo-American politicians try to get into the act, there is very little sausage left from Maddalena's hungry night at the airport. Michele has already shot off in anger, so Maddalena stays at Fenner's apartment. Michele decides to fix him and, when he does, Maddalena christens Michele with his own, well-aimed spaghetti and wrecks his restaurant. Released from hospital, Jock finds the ravishing Italian girl, and bourbon and ballads lead to bed. Next morning,

Jock's estranged wife turns up with the kids, plus Michele, repentant until Maddalena admits sleeping with the pressman. The men brawl and, maternal to the end, Maddalena puts Jock to bed with a lullaby before hailing a cab for Michele's apartment.

NOTES

They *must* compare notes. Then again, they cannot . . . Just as Sophia went fearlessly along the Mastroianni path with an Eduardo de Filippo play thinly disguised for the screen (his: *Shoot Louder, Louder . . . I Don't Understand*; hers: *Ghosts—Italian Style*), she now followed him solo-ing in New York, for an Italian director's eye-view of an Italian's life in the States (his: *Permette, Rocco Papaleo*; hers: *Lady Liberty*). None of them worked, except for middling success in Italy and the usual *parliamo italiano* import-territories. No doubt they should have made all four together.

The Pontis saw the New York movie as a distinct challenge, the first time back there with cameras since *That Kind of Woman*, two decades ago. The gamble was well backed up by the selection of a Mastroianni-tested director in Mario Monicelli, whose sketch had been dropped from *Boccaccio '70*. Also on the team, and for the first time due to his usual toil for Fellini, was Marcello's brother Ruggiero as editor.

Of Monicelli, Loren had high hopes: 'This is his first film with an American background. Maybe he can see things an American director cannot see any more because they are too accustomed to their own country. Maybe he can show sides of American life

American Return. Sophia films in the United States again. In New York only and strictly on her terms and in her language: defending the great Italian sausage from the U.S. Customs and her own fiancé, Luigi Proietti (bottom right), with the aid of newspaperman William Devane (left).

Fury. Sophia lets fly at Luigi Proietti in his restaurant. One plate of spaghetti coming up—and down, hard. Enter the cops.

that haven't been shown before: the humour, the loneliness, the confusion and wonder of a foreigner who comes to this country.'

Of her rôle, Maddalena: 'She is very close to what I generally feel. She comes to America from Naples. She is a strong, emotional woman. She doesn't accept falsities or compromises, and at times she has to pay very much for her truths. I would like to be able to live like that: to be sincere and honest all of the time, but sometimes you can't do that, sometimes you have to play the game.'

Hank Werba, *Variety*: 'Minus a co-star of equal or almost equal marquee impact in Mario Monicelli's sentimental satire comedy, Sophia Loren gives a semi-static performance in a series of composed frames obviously dedicated to her stunning facials. La Loren, however, is today no longer the plain, buxomy gal from a mortadella (sausage) plant in Bologna, but sleek and sophisticated—an enticing *femme fatale*. In *Mortadella*, she's snared between past image and present self.'

Respite. Sophia joins the Wanted lists. (*Lady Liberty*)

Shopping. Sophia and Luigi in Americana, Italian style.

White Sister

Bianco, Rosso e . . .
a.k.a. The Sin

1971

Italo-Franco-Spanish. Columbia-Warner. Champion (Rome)/Les Films Concordia (Paris)/Columbia Films (Paris)/Midega Films (Madrid)/C.I.P. (Madrid) co-production. *Director:* Alberto Lattuada. *Producer:* Carlo Ponti. *Executive Producer:* Gianni Cecchin. *Script:* Iaia Fiastri, Alberto Lattuada, Tonino Guerra, Ruggerio Maccari—*from a story by* Guerra, Maccari. *Photography:* Alfio Contini. *Editor:* Sergio Montanari. *Music:* Fred Bongusto. *Art Director:* Vincenzo del Prato. *Décor:* Ennio Michtettoni. *Sound:* Carlo Palmieri. *Assistant Director:* Mino Giarda. Technicolor. 96 minutes. [No. 5059]

CAST

Sophia Loren	*Sister Germana*
Adriano Celentano	*Annibale Pezzi*
Fernando Rey	*Chief Physician*
Juan Luis Galiardo	*Guido*
Luis Marin	*Libyan Brigadier*
Giuseppe Maffioli	*Dr. Arrighi*
Sergio Fasanelli	*Dr. Filippini*
Pilar Gomez Ferrer	*Sister Teresa*
Patrizia de Clara	*Sister Caterina*
Teresa Rabal	*Lisa*
Valentine	*Martina*
Tina Aumont	*Mrs. Ricci*
Bruno Niassibetti	*Ottolenghi*
Antonio Farina	*Valenzani*
Alessandra Mussolini	*Germana as a Child*
Ezio Curti	*Attilio*
Franio Curto	*Pinin*
Bruno Sciponi	*Chiacchi*
Massamiliano Filoni	*Giacomino*
Maria Marchi	*Giacomino's Mother*
Francesca Modigliani	*Lucia*
Carla Galletti	*Gina*

Some women give of themselves all there is to give...

COLUMBIA PICTURES presents
A Carlo Ponti Production

SOPHIA LOREN   ADRIANO CELENTANO
as
WHITE SISTER

with FERNANDO REY · JUAN LUIS GALIARDO and with TINA AUMONT
Screenplay by IAIA FIASTRI · ANTONIO GUERRA · ALBERTO LATTUADA · RUGGERO MACCARI
Directed by Alberto Lattuada   An Italo-French-Spanish Coproduction

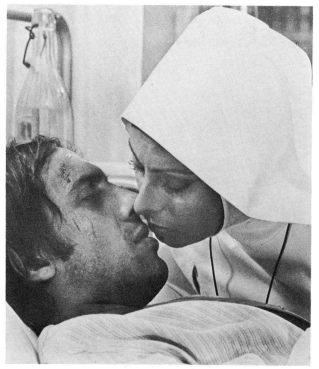

Bedside Manner. White Sister Sophia with red patient Adriano Celentano.

STORY

Following many years' service as a nursing nun in a missionary hospital in Libya, Sister Germana—who first took the veil after the traumatic death of her fiancé—returns to Northern Italy as chief nurse at a hospital outside Milan. The area is administered by the Communist Party, which is why—despite the tireless efforts of both Sister Germana and the chief physician—one Communist patient soon takes over the running of the entire place. This is Annibale Pezzi, an ulcerated working-man with an eye, and a hand, for the girls: with or without wimple. Far from being an ideal patient, he pokes his nose in most everywhere to the annoyance, and then interest, of the head nurse. Gradually she begins to understand, indeed sympathise with Pezzi and his ambitions to become a doctor. A relationship akin to love builds up: an impasse for both. It is only when he realises the depths of his own emotional entanglement, that Annibale agrees to be discharged and leaves . . . only to be killed in an accident.

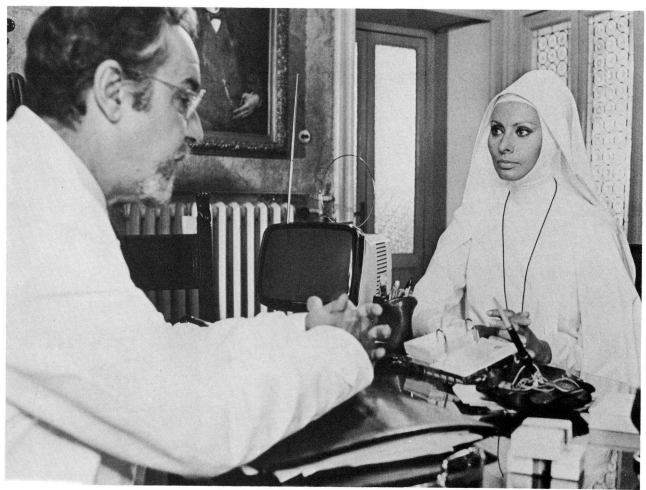

Conference. Sophia Loren with Fernando Rey.

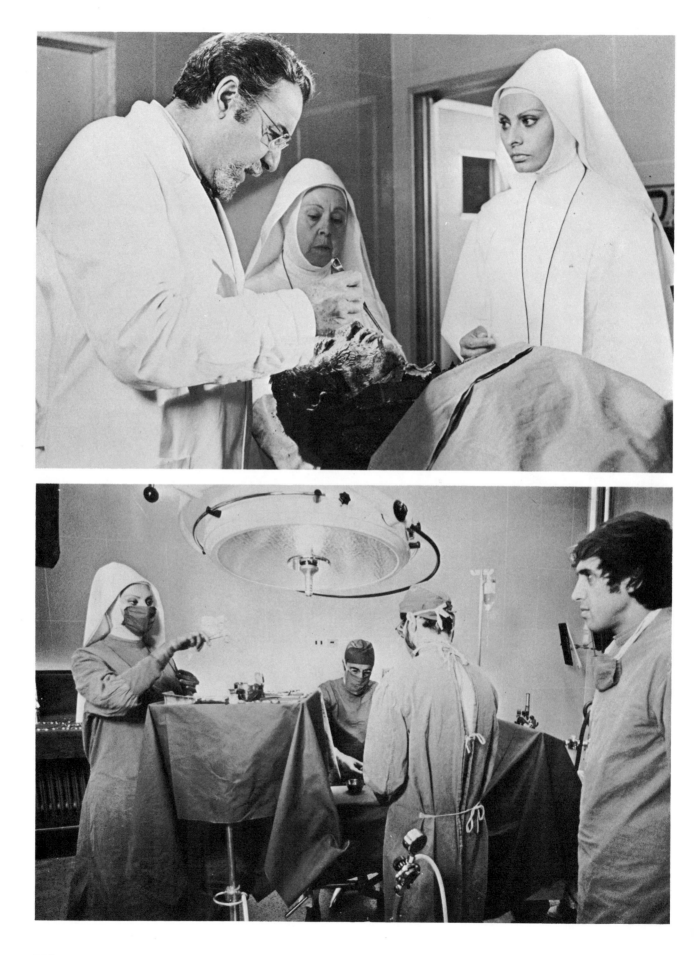

Operation. Dr. Fernando Rey at work, Sister Sophia assisting, Adriano Celentano waiting ...

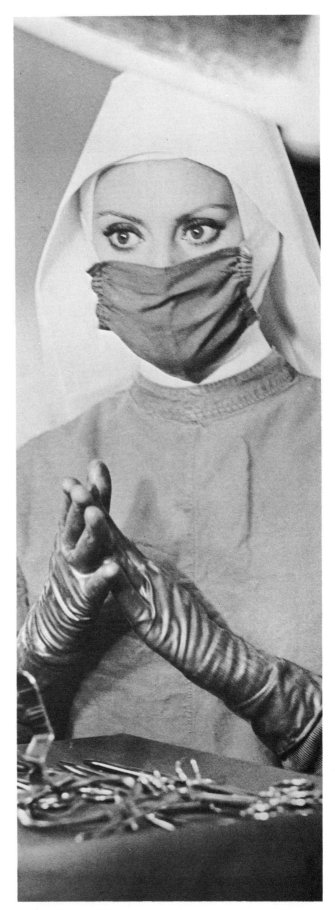

NOTES

After *The Priest's Wife*, ... *The Nun's Husband?* Nearly. Hang another ambition's scalp among the trophies. As most actresses, especially European, want to make a Western, they also have a prevailing need to play a nun. Loren first took the veil when considering the leading rôle in *The Nun of Monza* in the late '60s. She tested in costume, then left the project when Visconti withdrew his services. (A wise move in hindsight for both: Visconti's nephew Eriprando directed the film with an often very nude Anne Heywood as the tragic nun, who had still more tragedy heaped upon her history in the British release title of *The Awful Story of the Nun of Monza*.)

However, it is one thing for Italy to accept Sister Sophia, quite another for the world. Although made in 1971, this often quite humorous romantic melodrama remained unheard of as far as America was concerned until 1973, and at the time of going to press it still has not seen the light of British projection.

Too Italian? Maybe, but that has not prevented fully global releases of Loren movies before, many of which were entirely ethnic in premise and promise. Indeed, one State-side review, in *The Hollywood Reporter*, suggested *White Sister* was part of the fine tradition of the Italian neo-realist films of the '40s, '50s and '60s: 'a film style steeped in gregarious and heartrending performances and offering so much of the flavour of provincial Italy that one can almost smell the olive oil'.

The project went through the usual, current spate of title alterations—at least one per co-producing country and including the hardly apt *The Sin*. Italy kept the original, *Bianco, Rosso e ...* signifying Sister Sophia's white for the church, and red for her would-be doctor Communist admirer, Adriano Celantano. He is as successful on screen as he is on disc, providing comedy in the devious, one might say Mastroiannish, ways he avoids eviction from his hospital bed.

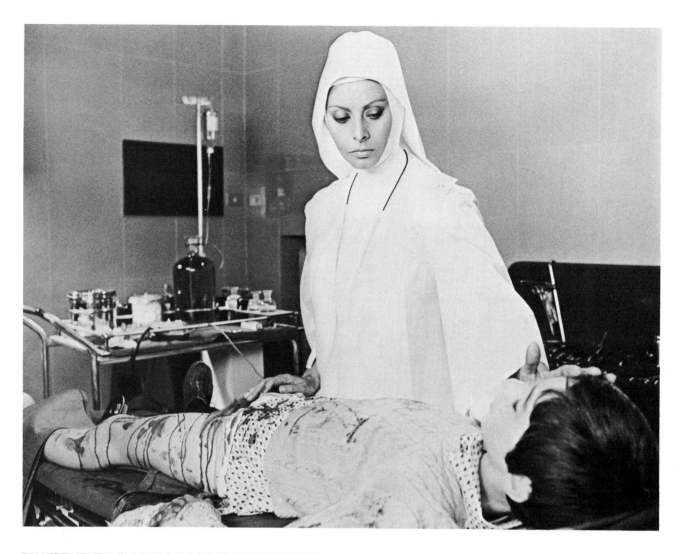

Linda Yellen, *The Hollywood Reporter*: 'A segment showing Annibale gazing at Miss Loren's hair, revealed to him for the first time (and that is all she reveals throughout the film), is invested with a romanticism and sensuality unequalled in the most explicit of movie love scenes ... Sophia Loren, whose beauty has always been incomparable but never before ethereal, proves herself, once again, to be an exceptionally accomplished actress, especially when dealing with the people and places she knows first-hand.'

Robert B. Frederick, *Variety*: '... a warm and sympathetic, if completely unbelievable story ... The audience that can believe the gorgeous Sophia Loren as a dedicated nun (complete with false eyelashes) will, however, be able to accept the wild machinations of the story.'

On a family note, Sophia's nun as a child is played by her niece, Alessandra Mussolini. A nice little child and, who knows, maybe an actress one day. Minus, though, the spur that made Aunty so great. Hunger.

Nun. Sophia becomes a nun after the death of her fiancé and spreads her love among her hospital patients.

Man Of La Mancha

1972

Italian. United Artists. P.E.A.: Produzioni Europee Associate production. *Director:* Arthur Hiller. *Executive Producer:* Alberto Grimaldi. *Associate Producer:* Saul Chaplin. *Script:* Dale Wasserman—*from the musical play by* Wasserman. *Photography:* Giuseppe Rotunno. *Editor:* Robert Jones. *Music Adapter/Conductor:* Laurence Rosenthal. *Décor/Costumes:* Luciano Damiani. *Make-Up:* Charles Parker, Euclide Santoli, Giuseppe Annunziata. *Hairstyles:* Amalia Paoletti, Ramon Gow, Ada Palombi. *Sound:* David Hildyard, Richard Portman. *Choreography:* Gillian Lynne. *Special Effects:* Adriana Pischiutta. *Songs:* 'Man of La Mancha'; 'It's All the Same'; 'Dulcinea'; 'Only Thinking of Him'; 'I Really Liked Him'; 'The Barbers' Song'; 'The Golden Helmet of Mambrino'; 'Little Bird, Little Bird'; 'The Impossible Dream'; 'The Dubbing'; 'Aldonza'; 'A Little Gossip'; 'Psalm'; 'The Quests'; *lyrics,* Joe Dariano; *music,* Mitch Leigh. Original production staged by Albert Marre; New York production by Albert W. Seldon, Hal James. DeLuxe color. 132 minutes.

CAST

Peter O'Toole	*Don Quixote de la Mancha* / *Miguel de Cervantes* / *Alonso Quijana*
Sohia Loren	*Dulcinea/Aldonza*
James Coco	*Sancho Panza*
Harry Andrews	*Innkeeper/Governor*
John Castle	*Sanson Carrasco/The Duke*
Brian Blessed	*Pedro*
Ian Richardson	*Padre*
Julie Gregg	*Antonia*
Rosalie Crutchley	*Housekeeper*
Gino Confortini	*Barber*
Marne Maitland	*Guard Captain*
Dorothy Sinclair	*Innkeeper's Wife*
Miriam Acevedo	*Fermina*

Dominic Barto, Poldo Bendani, Peppi Borza, Mario Donen, Fred Evans, Francesco Ferrini, Paolo Gozlino, Teddy Green, Peter Johnston, Roy Jones, Connel Miles, Steffan Zacharias, Lou Zamprogna—*Muleteers.*

STORY

Awaiting trial by the Inquisition in Seville for an offence against the Church, Miguel de Cervantes prepares an entertaining defence: the story of Don Quixote's campaign to restore the age of chivalry, aided in his windmill-tilting by Sancho Panza. At a wayside inn which Quixote insists is a castle, he annoys the obliging serving wench Aldonza by seeing her not as she is but as the Virginal Dulcinea. While his niece, housekeeper, padre and doctor consider how to deal with his madness, the Don admits he has never been knighted. The muleteers taunt

Musical. Loren's first musical since 1953, often reminiscent of *Two Women*.

Trio. James Coco, Peter O'Toole and Sophia bring Cervantes' classic characters to life: Sancho Panza, Don Quixote de la Mancha, and Dulcinea.

Quartet. Sophia and Harry Andrews double as Dulcinea and Aldonza and the Innkeeper and the Prison Governor.

Aldonza, and when Pedro claims her for the night, Quixote challenges him and knocks him down. The Don, Aldonza and Sancho win the pitched battle with the muleteers and Quixote is formally dubbed the Knight of the Woeful Countenance. Catching the old man's idealism, Aldonza ministers to the wounded, but they turn on her and carry her off; disillusioned she denounces the Don's dreams for bringing her fresh anguish. As expected by Quixote, the Dark Enchanter appears, his doctor in disguise; fantastically costumed as the Knight of Mirrors, he challenges the Don to combat, forcing him to see himself reflected as a fool and a madman. Quixote is defeated and Aldonza feels his loss as he departs. She follows him and pleads with the dying old man who called himself Don Quixote to become her chivalrous knight again. He rises to call for his armour and falls back, dead. 'A man died,' insists Aldonza, 'but Don Quixote is not dead.'

Armful. Sophia gives James Coco a bearhug after the combat sequence.

232

On-set. Sophia with director Arthur Hiller.

NOTES

'This is a challenge—I never have appeared in a musical before. I sing a little but I don't know yet if they will use my voice ... I hope I can, as it's very personal to me: to tell something by singing, to portray emotions in a song, this is very beautiful to me.'

And so it was. Although *Variety* moaned 'no songbird she', they did let her chant, quite beautifully (O'Toole was dubbed by Simon Gilbert). And so the actress who made her earliest impact miming to Renata Tebaldi's *Aida* arias finally found full opportunity to exercise her larynx on-screen. Yet another ambition. She had been working up to it in the comedy album with Sellers, the soundtrack album from her *Sophia Loren in Rome* TV show, and bouncy ballads in films right up to *Lady Liberty*.

As Aldonza, the begrimed Spanish beauty who sometimes goes upstairs with the men at the inn, and becomes ennobled in the demented ravings of the pixilated old Don, imagining her as his virginal lady-love, Loren had the kind of powerhouse acting and musical material to tug at her soul and our hearts. In her first number, 'It's All the Same', she laments her poverty and degraded sexual rôle in life —'one pair of arms is like another'; on to the dramatic denunciation of the Don's ideals in 'Aldonza'; and in the moving finale, she bids adieu to the dying knight with a reprise of 'The Impossible Dream'. This was the song—the only real hit of the show—that the publicity pushed; it also summed up the fate of the most expensive film of the year at $11,000,000.

Variety's Whitney Williams found the film musical, produced in the full-bodied style of the 1965 Tony and Drama Critics double-award-winning Broadway stage hit, was 'more a vehicle for musician than the narrative. It is needful of all the imagination the spectators can muster and it is frequently confusing ... Both Miss Loren and Coco give good accounts of themselves ...'

Time magazine's Jay Cocks also found her ravishing—'but she seems to be playing a kind of high-stepping version of *Two Women*'.

233

Combat. Peter O'Toole's frenzied Don swings a makeshift jousting pole at the muleteers taunting his idealised Dulcinea. She joins the fight with Sancho Panza and later binds the old man's head wounds.

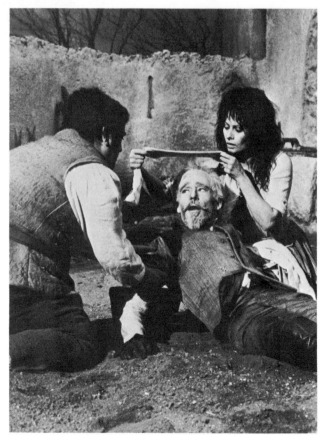

Taunts. The rugged muleteers tease Sophia Loren with a caustic version of the 'Little Bird' song.

Contempt. Furious at the jeering muleteers, Sophia's rattling, battling barmaid flings their food to the ground and sings her bitter lament, 'It's All The Same'.

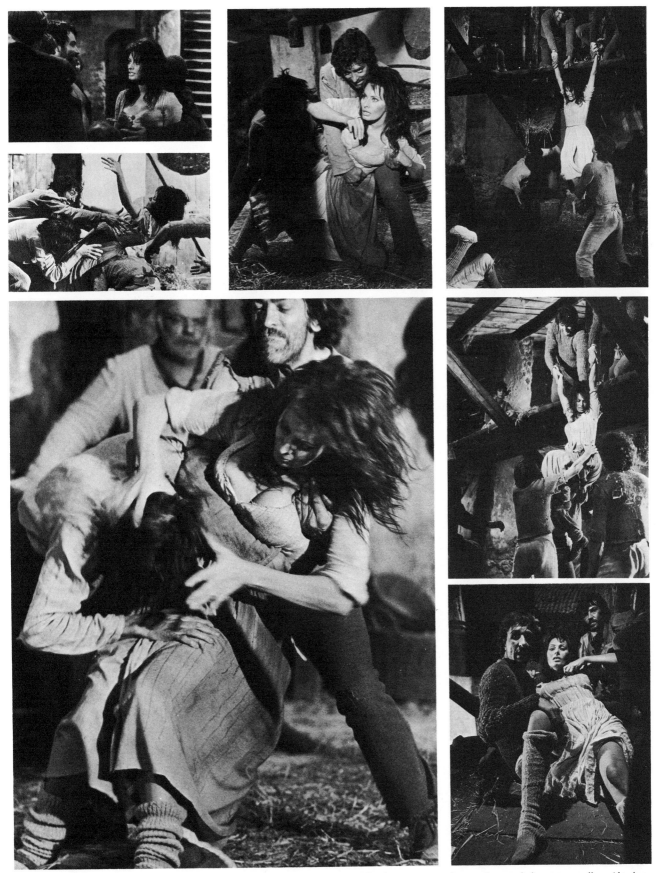

Assault. Sophia Loren turns the stage show's stylised choreographics into a more cinematic rough-house mauling. Having heard her praised by Don Quixote as his lady-love, the brawny muleteers abduct her from the inn, drunkenly intent on bringing her back down to their own animalistic level. The toughest musical since *West Side Story*.

Ideal. Sophia found Peter O'Toole a perfect screen partner—a combination she hopes to repeat.

Sophia Sings. In her first production number in the Dale Wasserman musical, Loren sings the bitter complaint that 'It's All The Same', 'one man's arms are like another'.

The Voyage

1973

Italian. United Artists. Champion production. *Director:* Vittorio De Sica. *Producer:* Carlo Ponti. *Executive Producer:* Turi Vasile. *Script:* Diego Fabbri, Massimo Franciosa, Luisa Montagnana—*from a novel by* Luigi Pirandello. *Photography:* Ennio Guarnieri. *Editor:* Franco Arcalli. *Music:* Manuel De Sica. *Production Design:* Luigi Scaccianoce. *Costumes:* Marcel Escoffier. *Sound:* Carlo Palmieri. *Assistant Directors:* Franco Cirino, Luisa Alessandri. *Production Manager:* Michele Marsala. Eastmancolor. 95 minutes. [No. 5679]

Unexpected. Loren tackles Pirandello.

CAST

Sophia Loren	*Adriana De Mauro*
Richard Burton	*Ceasare Braggi*
Ian Bannen	*Antonio Braggi*
Barbara Pilavin	*Signora De Mauro*
Annabella Incontrera	*Simona*
Paolo Lena	*Nandino*
Renato Pinciroli	*Dr. Mascine*
Daniele Vargas	*Notary Salierno*
Ettore Geri	*Renaldo*
Olga Romanelli	*Clementina*
Riccardo Mangano	*Dr. Carline*
Barrie Simmons	*Dr. De Paolo*
Franco Lauriano	*Notary's Clerk*
Antonio Anelli	*Puccini*

STORY

Sicily, 1912. A Sicilian widow cannot re-marry; especially not her brother-in-law. That is the code. Adriana and Cesare are much attracted, however. She has a serious heart ailment and Cesare leaves his rich orange groves and his mistress, Simona, to escort Adriana on a journey to various medical specialists. In Naples, a doctor advises them to enjoy to the full what time may be left to Adriana. To brighten her mood, Cesare takes the dazzled provincial girl to the first public entertainment she has ever been allowed to visit. Romantic Neapolitan songs, bursts of Offenbach and riotous can-cans in the *café-chantant* night club lift their spirits—and their glasses in a toast to the love they have always had for each other and which they now mean openly to declare. As the voyage continues for two years, Adriana awakens for the first time to life and love, until the romantic idyll concludes in Venice on the day Archduke Franz Ferdinand is assassinated in Sarajevo. For the lovers—as for the world—there can be no return to a more tranquil past.

NOTES

Sophia as a Sicilian—brought to life in Naples, meeting death in Venice. There seems to be some extra message in all this! Just as there was in De Sica also shooting in Milan, which holds a special affection in his artistic heart: he began his film

Heart Condition. Richard Burton takes sister-in-law Sophia Loren to a Palermo doctor, first stop in a search for a cure to her heart-trouble.

career there in 1932, shot *Miracle in Milan* there, as well as the *Today* episode in *Yesterday, Today and Tomorrow* and his more recent film, *A Brief Holiday*. Nothing, though, could be briefer than the subtly shaded tale of a suppressed love exploding as the young widow and her brother-in-law admirer seek a cure for her serious heart trouble so as to continue life and love—emanating from a novella by the Nobel Prize-winning Sicilian dramatist Pirandello. Except, of course, one of the future Loren assignments: *Brief Encounter*, itself.

Sophia is delighted with the production. 'Because it is not the kind of film they do nowadays, it goes really against the pornographic or sex films of today and I think it was worth making the attempt. It is a very romantic story, wonderfully made by Vittorio because he feels those kind of things deeply. And, on the screen, I must say Richard and I look very well together. It is very believable that we are in love. I am very pleased with our teaming because it is always so very difficult to find the right partner for me. Richard Burton—like Marcello Mastroianni and Peter O'Toole—is perfect!'

The film's musical score comes from the director's 24-year-old son, Manuel. The kin go on....

A journey is arranged to life itself—awakening the strictly-raised Sicilian woman to the pleasures of living, enjoyment, fun, music-hall and of love.

Family. Sophia Loren and screen-son; not, as everyone first thought, Carlo Ponti Jr. once more, but five-year-old Paolo Lena. Below, with British actor Ian Bannen.

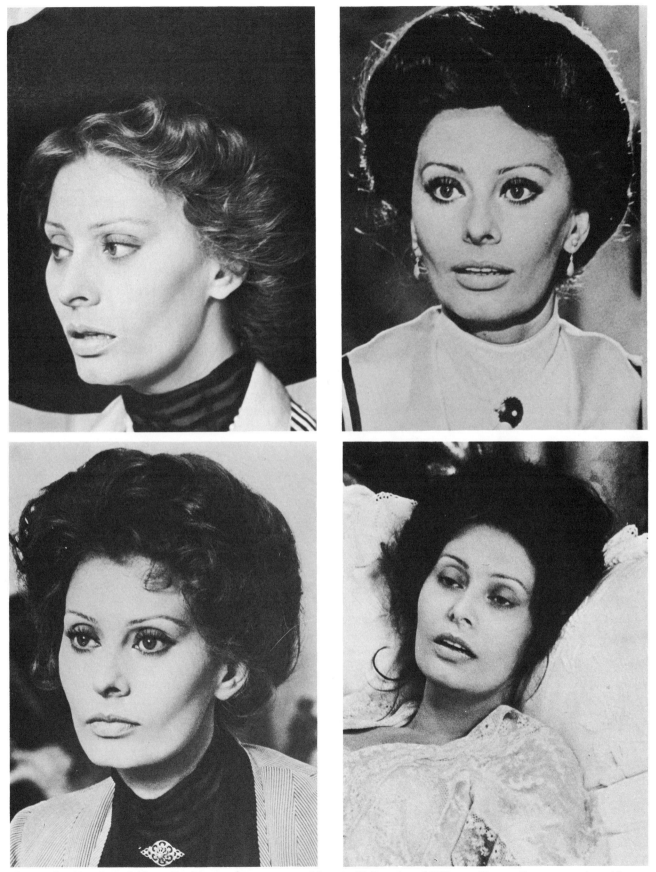

Faces. Sophia plays Adriana De Mauro: from weary widow in Sicily, circa 1912, to ailing mother, empassioned lover, 1913, and death in Venice, 1914.

Franco-Italian. Les Films Concordia (Paris)/Champion (Rome) co-production. *Director:* Andre Cayatte. *Producer:* Carlo Ponti. *Script:* Andre Cayatte, Henri Coupon, Pierre Dumayet, Paul Andreota. *Photography:* Jean Badal. *Editor:* Paul Cayatte. *Art Director:* Robert Clavel. *Production Manager:* Jacques Bourdon. Eastmancolor.

CAST

Sophia Loren	*Teresa Leoni*
Jean Gabin	*President Leguen*
Henri Garcin	*Maître Lannelongue*
Julien Bertheau	*Advocate General Verlac*
Michel Albertini	*Andre Leoni*
Gisele Casadessus	*Nicole Leguen*
Muriel Catala	*Annie Chartier*
Jean-Francois Remi	*Antoine Bertolucci*
Mario Pilar	*Joseph Sauveur*
Daniel Lecourtois	*The Public Attorney*
Francois Vibert	*Guichard*
Michel Robin	*Vericel, a Witness*
Maurice Nasil	*Cacharel, a Neighbour*

STORY

Lyon, October 1973. Andre Leoni is accused of the murder of Annie Chartier and is committed for trial. At the same moment, his mother Teresa Leoni turns up quite unexpectedly at the home of the President of the Assize Court, Judge Leguen.

Lyon, January 1974. Under various articles of the French Penal Code, Andre Leoni is liable for the death penalty. While the interventions of Counsel for the Defence, Maître Lannelongue, and of the Advocate General Verlac begin, the evidence of the neighbours and other witnesses drag on; the Public Attorney skirmishes with the President of the Bar; the personal relationship of Leguen and his wife Nicole evolves; and while all the normal trial proceedings continue, Teresa Leoni, cold-bloodedly and quite methodically, sets out to save the neck of her son by fair means or foul. Her plan is wild. She will force the judge to influence the jury by resorting to the ultra-modern fad of kidnapping and holding a hostage. The judge's wife ...

NOTES

This latest Loren rôle—her 70th rôle in 67 films in 24 years—seems to point the way she wants her major career to head in the future: 'to really push at the extremes of tragedy'. Teresa goes through all kinds of mental and physical hell in her mother's fight to have her son acquitted of a murder charge. 'She is convinced that her son is innocent and at the end, although he is acquitted, she finds he is guilty. Then, she kills herself. Because she can no longer believe in anything; everything in her life is messed up. She dies in a car accident. Deliberately? We do not really know but I can imagine that she puts herself in the spot to kill herself.'

The production was originally titled *La Tigresse et l'éléphant*—from the Kipling anecdote which declared that an elephant will always defeat a tiger in a fight, unless the tiger is a tigress, in which case both animals will die, monstrously intertwined. The judge is the elephant, out of sympathy with modern youth and about to preside on his last case before retiring; the tigress is the widow, defending the son she loves passionately. Director Andre Cayatte, a former lawyer himself and much addicted to legal premises, uses his scenario as an attack on the system of 'deep-seated personal conviction' of guilt or otherwise, and the resulting executory power in the hands of the courts, by demonstrating the influence of a particular judge's personality on the outcome of a case. He also aimed at exploring the jury's preconceptions about heredity. Playing the Advocate General in the case is Julian Bertheau, who also played Napoleon opposite Sophia's *Madame*.

Although the reviews are not yet in—the film is sight unseen at time of going to press—*Verdict* is likely to be more important to the French than to any other nation. Three months before shooting began in January 1974 her co-star Jean Gabin announced that his rôle of the judge would be his

Justice. Outside the Paris law courts where 'Mama' Loren fights like a tigress for a fair trial for her son by every means possible—including kidnapping the judge's wife.

adieu to the cinema. He was 70 on May 17, 1974. Sophia remains unconvinced of this fact, however. 'I tell you he has got such an energy that I do not think what he says is right. He adores being an actor. He adores making movies—92 in 40 years! He gets very excited and very nervous and everything that you can get when you adore still your profession—otherwise if this would be his last film, he would not care. He cares! He goes to see rushes. He looks at himself and says "I look good" or "I look bad"—he really cares. No, this man is a rock. He is an actor I have always admired; one of the most expressive and also one of the most outstanding in the history of the cinema. I do not think it is really his last film.'

Nor, of course, is it to be Sophia's farewell. 'If they would ask me to do things that I do not like to do, I think I would quit. But right now I am very excited about working. I like the films they make nowadays because they dare much more than they used to. When I do go, I would just retire, quietly steal away. No fuss, no Press conference saying this is going to be my last film. Because if by any chance after two or three years, something very interesting came up, you do not have to say "Well, you know, I've thought it over and decided to come back" ...'

Distraught. Sophia Loren as a mother with a teenage son (Michel Albertini) on trial for murder in Paris.

Confrontation. Jean Gabin endeavours to find where Loren has hidden his wife. His gun remains an empty threat: if he kills her, his wife will also die.

Retiring. Loren shares veteran French star Jean Gabin's farewell film.

Interrogation. Storming out of the trial after the judge's verbal attack on her son's gangster father, Loren lets fly at the Press and decides to save her boy her way.

Admiration Society. Gabin adored Loren and she remained convinced that he would not yet be able to completely withdraw from his movie career.

Death Wish. All belief in her son's innocence finally proved false, Sophia Loren drives to her death—in what constitutes the film's most shattering sequence, ending on a freeze-frame of Loren flying through the windscreen.

Honours List

1956. *Too Bad, She's Bad*
Best Actress, Buenos Aires festival.

1958. *The Key*
Best Actress Oscar, Japan.

1959. *Black Orchid*
Best Actress, Venice festival.
Best Actress David Di Donatello award, Taormina,
  Italy.
Victoire popularity award, France.

1960. *Two Women*
Best Actress Academy award, Hollywood, U.S.A.
Best Actress David Di Donatello award, Taormina,
  Italy.
Best Actress, Cannes festival.
Best Actress Critics' award, New York, U.S.A.
Best Actress, Cork festival, Eire.
Best Actress Oscar, Japan.
Best Actress Oscar, Belgium.
Best Actress Golden Owl, *Show Business Illustrated*,
  Chicago, U.S.A.
Best Actress Golden Globe, Hollywood Foreign
  Press, U.S.A.
Best Actress Trofeo Cinelandia, Spain.
Best Actress Ohio Critics, Cleveland, U.S.A.
Victoire popularity award, France.
Sole D'Oro popularity award, Italy.
Bambi popularity award, West Germany.
Prix Uilenspigoel, Fiammingo, Belgium.

1961. *Two Women* (continued)
A.P.P.C.B. Grand Prix Europa, U.S.A.
Best Actress, British Film Academy.
Best Actress Golden Laurel, Santiago, Chile.
Victoire popularity award, France.
Fungo D'Oro popularity award, Italy.

Heller in Pink Tights
Best Actress, Rapallo festival, Italy.

1962
Prix Uilenspigoel, Fiammingo, Belgium.
American Legion popularity award, U.S.A.
Bambi popularity award, West Germany.
Bravo popularity award, West Germany.
Victoire popularity award, France.
Snosiki popularity award, Finland.
Best Actress Premio Triunfo award, Spain.
Best Actress, Bengal Film Journalists' Association,
  Calcutta, India.

Popularity. Yet another Bambi award as the most popular foreign star in West Germany; Sophia Loren received eight Bambis during nine successive years.

1963
Bambi popularity award, West Germany.
Bravo popularity award, West Germany.
Snosiki popularity award, Finland.

1964
Bambi popularity award, West Germany.
Bravo popularity award, West Germany.
Snosiki popularity award, Finland.

Yesterday, Today and Tomorrow
Best Actress David Di Donatello award, Taormina,
  Italy.
Best Actress Golden Globe, Hollywood Foreign
  Press, U.S.A.

1965. *Marriage, Italian Style*
Best Actress David Di Donatello award, Taormina, Italy.
Best Actress Golden Globe, Hollywood Foreign Press, U.S.A.
Bambi popularity award, West Germany.
Bravo popularity award, West Germany.
Snosiki popularity award, Finland.
Prix Uilenspigoel, Fiammingo, Belgium.
Most Popular Actress, *Corriere della sera* newspaper referendum.
The Alexander Korda award for international star of the year, British Film Institute.

1966
Bambi popularity award, West Germany.
Snosiki popularity award, Finland.
Bravo popularity award, West Germany.
Texas Cinema Exhibitors' popularity award, U.S.A.
American Exhibitors' popularity award, U.S.A.

1967
Best Actress, Bengal Film Journalists' Association, Calcutta, India.
Bambi popularity award, West Germany.
Bravo popularity award, West Germany.

1968. *More than a Miracle*
Best Actress Ramo d'Oro award, Italy.
Box-office Favourite medal, Milan, Italy.
Bambi popularity award, West Germany.
Bravo popularity award, West Germany.

1969. *Marriage, Italian Style*
Best Foreign Actress diploma, U.S.S.R.

1970. *Sunflower*
Best Actress David Di Donatello award, Taormina, Italy.

1971
Best Actress, Bengal Film Journalists' Association, Calcutta, India.
Premio Stadio popularity award, Milan, Italy.

1972
Helene Curtis award, U.S.A.

1973
Simpatia popularity award, Italy.
Rudolph Valentino screen services award, Italy.

1974. *The Journey*
Best Actress David Di Donatello award, Taormina, Italy.

Awards. Bambis and Victoires galore, a Golden Globe and the first ever Alexander Korda trophy—the twenty-pointed gold star on the second shelf– but pride of place on the family shelves goes to the unique set of his 'n' her Hollywood Oscars: Carlo Ponti's for his production of *La Strada* and Sophia Loren's for her performance in *Two Women*.